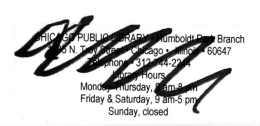

Praise for *Building the Latino Future*

Building the Latino Future takes you through the journeys of amazing Latinos Leaders who have redefined the American Dream and have succeeded on their "own" terms. Their lives and stories provide us with something we all need. . . . pure inspiration!"

—Yasmin Davidds, Consultant, Educator and Author

Building the Latino Future provides wonderful insight into how Latinos can effectively leverage their cultural heritage as an asset and yet still maintain their individuality. The examples shared in this book will surely help to create even more successful Latino professionals and leaders and will allow Latinos to make even larger contributions to society, academia and the workplace.

— Robert Rodriguez, PhD Chairman of the Board of Directors for the Hispanic Alliance for Career Enhancement and author of *Latino Talent: Effective Strategies to Recruit, Retain and Develop Hispanic Professionals*

BUILDING THE LATINO FUTURE

BUILDING THE LATINO FUTURE

Success Stories for the Next Generation

FRANK CARBAJAL
HUMBERTO MEDINA

WILEY

John Wiley & Sons, Inc.

Published by John Wiley & Sons, Inc., Hoboken, New Jersey
Published simultaneously in Canada

For general information on our other products and services or for technical support, please contact our Customer Care Department within the United States at (800) 762-2974, outside the United States at (317) 572-3993 or fax (317) 572-4002.

Wiley also publishes its books in a variety of electronic formats. Some content that appears in print may not be available in electronic books. For more information about Wiley products, visit our web site at www.wiley.com.

ISBN 978–0–470–22451–9
Printed in the United States of America

10 9 8 7 6 5 4 3 2 1

HUMBOLDT PARK

To our families and to the Latinos in the past that have paved the way for our future.

Contents

CONTENTS

CONTENTS

CONTENTS

FOREWORD: BUILDING THE LATINO FUTURE

It's an exciting time for the Latino community. According to the U.S. Census Bureau, Latinos are the fastest-growing minority in the country. By 2010, it is expected that Latino buying power will reach a trillion dollars. Latinos are taking increasingly visible roles in business, government, entertainment, and many other arenas, and are sitting on corporate boards, heading major companies, and serving as leaders in their communities.

These new Latino leaders have been blessed by the hard work of their parents and grandparents, most of whom were immigrants to the United States, who were willing to take positions as gardeners, janitors, busboys, and housekeepers, to create a better life for their children. Some worked two or three jobs, took public transportation, slept only three to four hours a day, and did whatever was required to make ends meet for their families.

If you are an immigrant or your parents are immigrants, this book will give you a whole new appreciation for your family's journey. If you are a business owner looking to gain insight into the Latino workforce, this book is a must. The practical knowledge you'll gain about Latino culture will help you understand your Latino associates. For example, you will learn that Latinos have a strong sense of community and prefer to work in teams rather than as individuals. You'll learn the important role spirituality plays in Latino success, and gain many other insights. The authors, Frank Carbajal and Humberto Medina, are well qualified to write such a book, as they are both Latino success stories in their own right.

The prominent Latinos featured in this book are eager to inspire successful new leaders by sharing their experiences, advice, and hope. There's a popular Spanish saying, "*Si se puede*," which means, "It can be done." That's perhaps the most powerful message in this book: It can be done, and you can do it!

—Ken Blanchard, coauthor of *The One-Minute Manager* and *The One-Minute Entrepreneur*

About the Authors

FRANK CARBAJAL

I spent most of my childhood in the barrio[1] of Meadow Fair in East San Jose, California, where my parents still live today. The streets of my old neighborhood are laid out like the keys of a piano, and are named after famous composers—Mozart, Puccini, Chopin, and so on. I remember the day Ms. Sanders, one of my grade school teachers, gave me a ride home because I had missed the school bus. As we turned onto my street, she looked over at me and said, "Did you know that the street you live on is named after Mozart, one of the most famous composers of all time?" She also explained to me about the layout of our neighborhood resembling a piano. I had never even thought about it, nor had anyone else I knew, so I was excited to share what I had learned with my parents and the members of my extended family, who lived with us at the time. It was

---

[1]For non-Hispanic readers, *barrio* is Spanish for neighborhood, but in U.S. Hispanic culture, it tends to take on a meaning similar to ghetto—that is, a low-income area with a population of similar ethnicity.

early recognition for me that, unfortunately, the only exposure to culture most *chavalitos* (kids)—as well as adult immigrants—in the barrio received was to that of the gang lifestyle—drug dealing and using, and early teen pregnancy. Very little emphasis was placed on education, and negative socioenvironmental influences made life a constant struggle for anyone who wanted to succeed.

For children in my barrio, as in many U.S. neighborhoods, it was difficult to acquire the desire to learn without family support and a strong foundation. By their early teens, those who weren't fortunate enough to be given that structure and supervision often drifted into gang banging and drug dealing. With the introduction of drugs and weapons into the "street culture," intragang violence and homicides spiraled out of control. Innocent bystanders often become victims. Today, the influence of such urban street gangs is compounded by widespread media exposure. In particular, certain rap artists who were former gang members have glorified their past by writing songs about it. Some of these records sell by the millions to young listeners worldwide, making the gang lifestyle even more appealing to disenfranchised youth. This phenomenon makes it even more vital to provide mentoring programs and introduce other positive and valuable resources into the barrios.

In my own case, my father was determined to protect me from these negative influences. Thus, my working life started at eight years old. Every summer, my parents showed my four siblings and me the value of a work ethic by taking us out to pick cherries, apricots, and, at times, strawberries, in what was then called Santa Clara Valley (now nicknamed Silicon Valley). The most difficult part of the day for me was waking up between 4:30 and 5:00 A.M. and getting ready to head out for another long day of manual labor. I vividly remember splashing water on my face to wake up, since I was too young for coffee. Without a word of complaint or rebellion, all five of us would pack into our father's 1978 pink Datsun, with silver flames along the side. We didn't bother with seat belts, but I felt safe, because I was with my parents and siblings. This job taught me early to be respectful of migrant workers, regardless of their nationality. The men and women in the fields of the Santa Clara Valley were my father's friends, and they were the *jefes*, the bosses of the field.

My father also worked part-time for a janitorial service company, in addition to working full-time at a cannery. On the weekends, I went with him, helping to clean offices. I know that my father's intent was to keep me busy on weekends and in the summers, in order to keep me away from some of the bad kids in the barrio. I believe his motive was also to make me realize the significance of an education. He didn't want me to work as hard as he had to; he wanted me to work smarter. My parents were much like the increasing number of immigrants who come to America: they made sacrifices to provide their children with a better lifestyle.

Those weekends spent working with my father inspired me to believe that one day I could graduate from high school, go to college, and ultimately have an office of my own, like the ones I spent so many hours cleaning. I remember once daydreaming as I was cleaning the office of the CEO of a very successful tortilla company. I vividly recall slowly pushing the vacuum cleaner as I admired everything in the office, from the rich smell of mahogany to the awards of recognition he received as an outstanding Latino. I also enjoyed looking at his recreation rewards hanging on the wall, and the ticket stubs from a Super Bowl the San Francisco 49ers played in, which were carefully displayed in a case. My father walked in and interrupted my reverie, shouting, "*Hijo* (son), this is the reason you need to concentrate in school, and concentrate on going to college. This isn't the type of job cut out for you. I don't want you to work like a *burro* (donkey)."

My parents were only able to complete their elementary education, since they had to start working to help support their families when they were very young. They didn't want me to follow that same path. My father shared the stories and experiences he had living in a camper or a tent out in campgrounds, so that he could work to pick the crops and earn a living.

My father demonstrated his emotional support and unconditional love for me by helping me make decisions about which kids to avoid in the barrio, and by reminding me to focus on my education rather than spending my time with the wrong crowd. Thanks to my parents' encouragement, I became the first in my family to go to college; I graduated with a bachelor's degree in social work and, later, a master's degree in human resources management. Though these were great accomplishments, I still lacked a direction about what to do next. Fortunately, I found my first mentor in a man named John Tweeten, an extraordinary man who believed I could make a difference by working with Latinos.

HUMBERTO MEDINA

My family came to the United States almost thirty years ago, looking for a better life. My mother was looking for a new start after her divorce, and decided to move from Venezuela to Arlington, Virginia. My first memory of the United States is of arriving alone a few months after my mother, and having to talk to the immigration officer at JFK airport. I had a few basic English classes under my belt, and I was an avid listener of American radio programs in Venezuela, so I was confident in my ability to speak English. That confidence lasted just about three minutes, until the officer looked at me with a funny face and signaled me to follow him to the secondary inspection area, where my English vanished as I struggled to answer his questions. Where were my parents? Why was I traveling alone?

As it turned out, getting through immigration with my student visa and enrolling in English classes at Wakefield High School in Arlington were the easy steps to starting my life in this country, for in 1987, the Venezuelan economy collapsed and my father was no longer able to afford the money he had been sending each month to help us. My mother then tried for many months to get a job to keep us here. She hoped to be a secretary, but the only job she found was as a maid in a small hotel. My heart ached to see her leave the apartment early each morning, only to return late, exhausted, and still have to make dinner and take care of us. After a few months of making do with very little, my mother lost all hope and strength, and she and my sisters decided to return to Venezuela.

As for me, I had the crazy idea of staying alone and making something of my life in the United States. Somehow, I felt this was the only chance I had, and so I began my new life without my family. I took many odd jobs to try to stay afloat—I worked as a painter, limo driver, truck packer, photographer, and even as Chucky at a Chucky Cheese franchise. I learned many important lessons in the school of hard knocks at that time. My mom worried constantly about having left me behind, whereas my dad thought I would return to Venezuela after getting a good dose of reality.

But I had managed to remain here, and with plenty of encouragement from my folks, I studied to pass the GED. Soon after, I headed for community college to enter a computer engineering program—although I didn't have the money I needed to enroll. My father swore that we would find a way to pay for my education if I was able to get into the program. However, balancing college and full-time work was not as easy as I expected, and soon I was trying to convince my father that instead of helping me pay for college, he should give me the money to invest in my own business career. After all, I was in the land of entrepreneurship.

After a few days of negotiating with my father, he agreed to lend me the money, but only on the condition that it would come out my education fund. I would have to make the money up myself if I decided to go back to college if I failed in my entrepreneurial efforts.

My first business venture began with the purchase of a car that needed some repairs, which I made, so that it passed inspection. I cleaned it up, then published an ad to sell it in the *Washington Post*. I had purchased the car for $450, put another $200 into it, and after two weeks sold it for $1,600 to the second person who responded to the ad. I remember thinking, wow, that was easer than working forty hours a week! If I could make this happen twenty times a month, I would be set. A few years later, I leased a lot after getting a license to sell cars. It was a one-acre lot, large enough to hold sixty units. Eventually, I had up to twelve people working for me. So, at the age of twenty-two, I was making more than any of my friends at school, and I could drive a different car every day if I wanted to. Even my father was impressed enough to travel here to see my business firsthand.

Nevertheless, my friends and family continued to push me to go back to school. So, when I was twenty-five, I decided to sell my part of the business and make getting an education my top priority. I had saved enough and my dad was still willing to help; plus, the federal government was also ready to lend a hand with student loans. I also became the oldest recipient of a Spanish Scholarship from a Latino Organization in Washington, DC—which I could hardly believe was real until I made out the check to George Mason University.

I also got myself a job with a catering business in the area, one that gave me flexible hours, allowing me to attend school. The best part of the job was that I had the chance to serve many important people in the four years I worked in the Washington political scene, some whom left big impressions on me, especially actress Susan Sarandon and former President George H.W. Bush.

At school, I became very focused, and got my bachelor of arts degree in psychology in just three years. I immediately enrolled in graduate school and earned my Master of Science degree in organizational development from the American University. This master's program opened important doors in my life. There I met a community of professionals who have played an important role in my career. At school I also had the good fortune to sit next to a beautiful redhead, Debbie Blanchard, who later became my wife. Through knowing Debbie I got the chance to work for Ken Blanchard, a wonderful mentor who has helped me grow immensely, both professionally and spiritually. Today, I lead The Ken Blanchard Companies' Latin American Division, where I have the extraordinary opportunity to help the next generation of Latin workers in my motherland become better leaders.

As I look back on the development of this book, I realize that, like many of the people whose stories are told in this book, I have also benefited from the FUTURE acronym that we now share with you. I too decided to get laser-focused on what I wanted to do. In overcoming adversity and challenges, I have come to rely on a network of professionals and friends who are always there to help me, and I become more successful as I continue to learn, teach, and share my experiences with others.

I have always strongly believed that hope was the glue that held everything together for me when I decided to stay in the United States on my own. Hope is the first thing that we bring to life. As we come to life, our parents are filled with hope that all will be well with us and that we will be successful in life. As we grow and learn, we hope to be successful ourselves. Once we graduate from college or graduate school, we hope to be able to manage and execute the mission and goals of the organization or company that hires us.

Once we become leaders, we then carry the hopes of our organization, as well as the people who work for us—leaders are the keepers of hope for organizations and the people who work for them. Our team hopes that we can carry out the company strategy, while also helping them grow and fulfill their individual goals. The ultimate objective is to instill hope in others for the future, as the great leaders have done, leaders like Nelson Mandela, Martin Luther King, Jr., and Simon Bolivar. Theirs was a leadership of service and hope for coming generations. Their leadership transcended their physical existence into our own.

I can't say that I am anywhere close to "transcending hope" with this book, but I surely appreciate the opportunity of carrying on the promise for this country. Thank you all for the opportunity of sharing my dreams and hopes with you!

~~~

Our personal experiences impelled us to write this book, to share the success stories of Latino leaders throughout the United States, men and women who have risen to the top in their respective professions and have become proactive in creating their future today. We hope that you will be inspired to follow in their footsteps, that you too will find your own way to help "build the Latino future" at the same time you make your own dreams come true.

INTRODUCTION

The Future Leadership Model

This book is the result of a series of interviews with fifty-nine individuals who have each overcome obstacles to reach their dreams of success. Throughout the success stories told by these individuals were common threads: each contained elements of six key principles—focus, unity, tenacity, unique ability, resiliency, and education. To explain these key principles of success, we have created the FUTURE Leadership Model. This model is not meant to be a sequential, step-by-step process, because each element is interconnected with, and strengthened by, the others. Rather, it is a tool for increasing your chances for success, gaining perspective, and determining what is lacking in your effort to reach your goals.

Each letter of the FUTURE Model represents a strength a successful person needs to possess. When combined, these strengths can be used as a guideline for reaching your goals and success.

Focus: Focus Your Strengths and Energy

When you clarify your goals and objectives, you create a positive flow of energy that will help you fulfill your dreams of success. Focus gives you a sense of purpose and enables you to be clearer about who you are. In several of the personal accounts in this book, you will learn how the individuals maintained their focus, at the same time they remained flexible to inevitable changes in their plans. They took advantage of opportunities that came their way and never lost sight of their ultimate goal.

Without focus, how can you know where you are going? It has been said that those who do not have a goal are used by those who do. If you do not have your own goals, you will end up working toward someone else's goal. Without focus, your ability to lead will not get you where you want to go.

Unity: Unity and Community Are Key

Unity is essential in life and for success. No one, no matter how focused, can achieve success by themselves. All successful people are empowered by a network of peers, which helps them to get ahead and achieve success. It goes without saying that an individual becomes more powerful with the support of others. However, you must seek out these support networks; they will not come looking for you.

Everyone needs two networks. First is the one composed of your family and friends, which you may tend to take for granted—don't! The second network comprises peers, colleagues, role models, and mentors, those you seek out and rely on for professional advice and support; people you admire and want to emulate. Surrounded by such a network gives you reliable sources for collaboration and brainstorming, which in turn lead to further clarity of goals and direction.

TENACITY: TENACITY BUILDS CHARACTER AND HUMILITY

Each of us must persevere in order to reach our personal goals; we must learn to be tenacious, for doing so builds our character and keeps us humble. As you will see throughout this book, all of the individuals profiled had to work hard and overcome obstacles before they achieved success. Neither athletic champion nor political leader nor corporate executive achieved his or her success right away.

Approach your goals with by balancing tenacity and humility. When you do so, you will be better equipped to face challenges, and you will learn when to be patient and when to be assertive. Just as important, you will learn to get out of your own way.

Ken Blanchard, noted author and inspirational speaker, has often said that humility is not thinking less of yourself, but thinking of yourself less. Being humble gives you staying power, an ability to endure while you evaluate your situation, and assess what needs to be done to move forward.

In conducting the interviews for this book, we also found that successful people know how to be patient—they learned never to give up.

UNIQUE ABILITY: EVERYONE HAS A UNIQUE STRENGTH

We are all unique in some way. To succeed, first determine what comes naturally to you and what you do better than anyone else; then focus on that unique ability and build on it. By connecting your skills to your goals in this way, you learn more about yourself, and are therefore better able to make the most of your gifts at the same time you learn where you need strengthening or improving. Learn to draw energy and momentum from your strengths. Build on that energy and focus on those areas where you are strongest.

There is a powerful connection between strength and passion. Those things that you are naturally good at are most likely the things you are also passionate about. Successful people draw on this combined source of energy to achieve their goals.

RESILIENCY: RESILIENCY BUILDS STRENGTH

Learning how to bounce back from adversity is a necessary ingredient of success. All the successful people profiled in this book demonstrated resiliency—the ability and willingness to recover from setbacks. Such resiliency, of course, requires focus and tenacity, as already described.

When successful people hit an obstacle or are thrown off course, they look at the situation as a learning experience. They might ask what they have learned not to do, or what to do differently, to avoid a similar obstacle in the future. The knowledge they gain from introspection, and from evaluating the setback honestly, gives them the strength to push on. Resiliency emerges when you learn to incorporate the knowledge gained from setbacks into your future actions.

EDUCATION: EDUCATE OTHERS AND GROW WITH THEM

Without exception the individuals profiled in this book point to the importance of education in achieving their success. They also stress the importance of passing their knowledge along, and to helping others become educated themselves. When you teach others, you are likewise taught by them. So teach, but also be teachable—when you stop learning, you stop growing. If your education ends with you, you will leave nothing behind to sustain future generations.

A vital aspect of education is mentoring. Look for mentors everywhere, in your family, your community, your schools, churches, even on the street.

Then return the favor: be a mentor. An integral part of success is to help others by sharing your strengths and passion. Keep the success going and growing, beyond yourself.

INTO THE FUTURE

As you can see, the six elements of the FUTURE Model are integral to one another; they combine to provide a person with balance and direction to a clearer path to success. Each of the individuals interviewed for this book exhibit, to varying degrees, how these concepts can work in practice. They also demonstrate how to use them not just for the benefit of the individual but for the greater good as well. To be truly successful, we believe you must be equally strong in all six areas.

I

FOCUS

Focus begins with an examination of yourself and your surroundings. Examine your dreams and desires. What do you want to accomplish? What are you passionate about? To what are you willing to dedicate time and energy to achieve? If you are unhappy with where you are, where would you rather be? If you have your sights set on success, what does that success look like? What will you need to get there?

Choosing a goal is independent of background or situation. Ultimately, these things do not matter. If elements of your background or situation will likely impede your success, identify those barriers and find ways around or over them. You must have discipline and concentration to determine your focus. It is equally important that you share your goals with others, to allow for the necessary synergy of your network and to encourage a flow of positive energy.

Once you have identified your goal, you can determine your areas of focus. With focus, you can avoid distractions and proceed toward your goal despite negative influences. Concentrating all your energy on your goal or purpose is crucial to success. Imagine putting yourself in a position in which you are homed in on a specific goal or purpose, without being distracted by anything outside that purpose. Everyone is capable of tapping into personal self-discipline, enabling them to find the "zone" and stay there, ultimately reaching their goals.

Maintaining self-discipline requires avoiding negative influences and distractions, focusing on succeeding at what is right for right now, and not being dissuaded by criticism. Focus requires being truthful about where you are and what you want. It is about making a choice.

The individuals whose stories we spotlight in this section made a choice. For them, that choice was the beginning of their journey to success. They found determination and had the heart to withstand criticism.

Another way to focus your energy is to put your passion into play. The key is to look within yourself and focus on the things that motivate you most in life. Do something that comes naturally to you, and do it with confidence. That kind of focus and drive, critical to success in Hollywood or when careening down the hills in a Winter Olympics luge competition, fuels and is fueled by passion. It is our inner drive that makes us work toward our goals and concentrate on our solutions.

The concept of focus means different things to different people. The subjects of the stories in this section exhibit different aspects of focus. Although each applied a different focus strategy to achieve his or her goals, collectively their successes serve as an example of how to gain clarity about one's own goals. Whether as a result of tapping into a zone, disregarding criticism, or recovering after a change in circumstances, they all established a clear sense of their goals.

1

Self-Discipline Is Key

EDWARD JAMES OLMOS
Actor, Director, and Community Activist

Maintaining self-discipline requires avoiding negative influences
and focusing on succeeding at what is right for right now.

Edward James Olmos remembers his grandfather walking him to Belvedere Elementary on the first day of school and reading to him what was written on the archway they walked under: "If it isn't said in English, it isn't worth saying at all." This insensitive statement didn't discourage Spanish-speaking Olmos. Instead, it empowered him to be proud of his roots and never forget who he is.

Olmos was born on February 24, 1947, and was raised in an underprivileged area of East Los Angeles, California. His father had left Mexico City, Mexico, at a young age, with nothing more than a sixth-grade education. After settling in Los Angeles, his father beat the odds and returned to school, proudly earning his high school diploma. Olmos' mother left school after the eighth grade, but she, too, returned to school to complete her education after her children were grown. Education was always an important goal for the Olmos family.

The Olmos believed their children should be involved in sports as well, as a means of staying out of trouble and developing self-discipline. Edward James and his father believed he would become a professional ball player one day, but when he was fifteen years old, he changed his mind about his career goal. Olmos decided he wanted to become a singer and dancer. His family respected his choice and supported his decision. By the time he graduated from high school, Olmos and his band, Pacific Ocean, was playing regular engagements at the top nightclubs in Los Angeles.

"To maintain self-discipline, remind yourself to avoid distractions at work or play."

Edward James Olmos realized early on that self-discipline is a key element of success. Succeeding in Hollywood, as in any industry, takes focus and determination. Self-discipline provides focus and direction, but it is self-generated; it is up to an individual to focus on his or her goals. Distractions are inevitable in busy lifestyles, but the key to self-discipline is staying composed and listening to one's inner voice, always being cognizant that the distractions of one's life can cause setbacks, and that being disciplined is the key to staying on track.

Olmos remembers the inspiration he received from his parents and grandparents. They told him that he was capable of succeeding at anything he set his mind to. And so he set his mind to being successful in Hollywood. It takes focus and discipline to accomplish what Olmos has in the film industry. Edward James Olmos has become a great star, with such films as *Blade Runner*, *Stand and Deliver*, *Mi Familia*, and *Selena*, and the TV series, *Battlestar Gallactica*, to his credit.

"Create your goal, find the discipline, and stay on track."

2

Thinking for the Electronic Age

Dr. Hector Ruiz
CEO and Chairman of Advanced Micro Devices

Be passionate about what comes naturally to you.

To see him now, a successful electronic engineer, appointed by President George W. Bush to serve as one of his advisors on issues of technology and scientific research, one would never know that Dr. Hector Ruiz comes from very humble beginnings.

Dr. Ruiz was raised in Piedras Negras, Mexico, a town whose name means "Black Rock" in English. It was a busy, modern town, with a large part of its economy based on tourism, mostly people visiting from Texas. As the name implies, Piedras Negras, began as a coal-mining town; but by the 1960s, the coal mines were no longer the main source of income, largely due to an increasing number of American companies investing in the area.

Dr. Ruiz remembers fondly the town that played a part in instilling good values in him and helping to shape his future. His parents, Gregorio and Maria, were very humble and righteous people, in that they believed that doing what was right was important. They became young Hector's role models, teaching him always to do things with pride and integrity. Even as a young boy, Hector grew up with the strong feeling that he understood, at least within the context of Latino culture, what was right and what was wrong, what was important and what was trivial, and how to make those distinctions. His parents taught him to not only to be a loving person, but also how to discern for himself what was right and what was wrong. Hector looks back on his childhood as an inspiring time, which laid the foundation for his accomplished adulthood.

"Pride and integrity start at home."

As a teenager, Hector worked hard as a shoeshine boy. Hector always showed passion for any type of work he did, however modest. People saw the glimmer of hope and ambition in his eye. When Hector was about fourteen years old, he met Olive Given, a Methodist missionary woman who lived near his parents. She would often ask Hector to run errands for her, in an effort to make a connection with Hector and teach him English. Hector shared with Olive his passion for automotive mechanics, and she encouraged him to pursue what he was passionate about, telling him that it was good to be enthusiastic about things that you can do well.

But the key to success in America, she told him, was to learn English. Hector wanted to impress her, so he studied English on his own and read countless books. The next thing he knew, Olive was walking Hector across the border to a high school in Eagle Pass, Texas. Crossing the border didn't entail much of a cultural difference, with the exception that the schools expected students to speak English.

"Hard work and perseverance pay off every time."

At this point, Hector was in his late teens, and still wasn't proficient in English. It was nerve-wracking, then, that his first English assignment was to write an essay. Not only was Hector unfamiliar with the curriculum in general, but he had never written an essay before. He remembers doing the best he could with his limited knowledge of English and turning in his essay. But he received a failing grade. Fortunately, his teacher, also a Latino, did not dismiss the struggling student. Instead, he worked with Hector, until Hector became proficient in English, eventually earning an "A." Hector was also exceptionally talented in science and math.

So, with hard work and perseverance, and a little help from his English teacher, he eventually graduated as valedictorian.

Thus, Hector learned early that in order to be successful, you must also put in the time and effort. He gives much of the credit for his early success to the principal and teachers at his school in Eagle Pass, and especially to Olive Given. As you can imagine, in the 1960s giving a chance to a young Mexican from a border town was not only considered unacceptable, but was also unheard of. It was a radical idea at the time to allow a small number of Mexican youth to attend school in that Texas town, and Dr. Ruiz counts himself fortunate to have been one of those few.

"Dream as if you're going to live forever, but act as if you're going to die tomorrow."

Dr. Ruiz went on to earn bachelor's and master's degrees in electrical engineering from the University of Texas-Austin and a doctorate in electronics from Rice University. He joined Advanced Micro Devices (AMD) in 2000, and was appointed chairman of the board in 2004. In 2007, President Bush appointed Dr. Ruiz to serve on the President's Council of Advisors on Science and Technology (PCAST), a group composed of 23 leaders from the private sector, as well as academic and research communities, who advise the president on issues related to technology, scientific research priorities, and math and science education. In addition, Dr. Ruiz currently serves on the National Security Telecommunications Advisory Committee (NSTAC), which provides industry-based advice and expertise to the president on issues and problems related to implementing national security and emergency preparedness communications policies. And as one of the leaders in the technology sector, Dr. Ruiz is also helping the Latino community become proficient in this area.

At the annual Clinton Global Initiative, CEOs make public commitments to solve world problems. In the past, more than 262 were made, valued at more than $7.3 billion, benefiting more than 500 organizations and helping people in more than 100 countries. Past speakers of the Internet Caucus Advisory Committee Speaker Series have included Internet founding fathers Vint Cerf, Tim Berners-Lee, and Marty Cooper, as well as industry leaders Bill Gates, Michael Eisner, and Meg Whitman. In March 2006, Dr. Hector Ruiz joined this company of giants. To date, Latinos represent less than 1.5 percent of the leadership roles in Fortune 500 companies, but this is beginning to change, as more and more Latinos are filling executive positions. Dr. Ruiz is one of those, and as such, serves as a sign of the times.

3

Never Be Afraid to Succeed

AIDA ALVAREZ
Former Administrator, U.S. Small Business Administration

Leadership happens in the blink of an eye.

Chances are, if in recent years you had the opportunity to obtain a small business loan from the United States Small Business Administration (SBA), and you happen to be a woman or a minority, your loan application was influenced by Aida Alvarez.

In 1997, Aida was sworn in as the twentieth SBA administrator under President Clinton's administration, and in so doing made history as the first Latina, and the first Puerto Rican, to direct the SBA, a White House cabinet position. The SBA is the nation's largest single backer of small business loans worth more than 45 billion dollars. In her position as administrator, Aida provides guidance to the SBA in processing the applications of those who are not typically funded, namely women and minorities.

A few years earlier, in 1993, Aida became the first director of the Office of Federal Housing Enterprise Oversight (OFHEO). In this position, she managed the Federal National Mortgage Association, Fannie Mae, and Fannie Mac. The latter two are the nation's largest finance companies, leading the trillion-dollar secondary mortgage markets and providing home loans to individuals who are usually denied them from first-rate banks—again, most commonly, minorities.

Before reaching the top at the SBA and OFHEO, Aida gained valuable work experience in the business and banking industry. For seven years, she worked in public finance in New York, and then for Bears Stearns and Boston Corporation in San Francisco, where she led a team of bankers in marketing and tax-exempt bond issues.

Aida was born in the northwestern seaport town of Aguadilla, Puerto Rico, but was raised in New York City. Growing up in the Big Apple was tough at times—literally. Aida recalls, when she was only twelve years old, being forced to fight a girl who was in a gang. Instead of giving in to peer pressure, however, Aida backed out of the fight. Surprisingly, Aida was declared the winner for being the smarter of the two, and subsequently was asked to be part of the gang, which she graciously declined.

"Don't be afraid, and never give up.

Aida, a bright girl, was a straight-A student at St. Joseph's Catholic School. But as at most urban schools, Latinos at St. Joseph's were encouraged to attend trade school upon graduation. Latinas, in particular, were encouraged to become secretaries.

Luckily for Aida, one of the nuns, Sister Ramona, saw the amazing potential in Aida and encouraged her to set her sights on attending college. Her stellar grades gained her admission to the Aspira (Inspire) Program at Yale University. There, Aida's academic gifts caught the eye of Charlie McCarthy, who convinced her to apply to Radcliffe. At first, the idea of attending such a prestigious university intimidated Aida—who told McCarthy a high-caliber university education was only for the "rich kids." But with his encouragement, she applied and was accepted. Aida graduated cum laude in 1971.

Looking back on her accomplishments, Aida Alvarez has this advice for any young person facing a similar journey: "Don't be afraid, and never give up. If you've taken a risk, even if you think you've lost, you've actually really won!"

4

Downhill at 85 Miles Per Hour

RUBEN GONZALEZ
Three-Time Olympic Luge Athlete and Author

*Speeding downhill at 85 miles per hour on a luge course requires focus,
and zoning in on your very best form of concentration.*

Imagine driving down the freeway at 85 miles per hour. At that speed, it is just as important to pay attention to the other drivers and the road conditions as it is to your own body and behavior. If you don't—if your eye leaves the road for a second, to change the track on the CD player or to look in the rearview mirror at a passenger in the back seat—the results could be disastrous. To stay safe driving at that speed, the driver must zone in on the situation and concentrate on everything that is happening.

Now imagine traveling 85 miles per hour, paying close attention to your driving as well as to the other drivers on the road, but in a luge sled instead of a car, and imagine that the road you are traveling down at that speed is not a paved freeway but an icy track. Olympic athlete Ruben Gonzalez does not need to imagine this scenario: he lived it every day.

The story of Ruben Gonzalez is one of inspiration. His life began with rejection and isolation. He didn't have many friends growing up, and as a young boy, dreamed of becoming a professional soccer player. He remembers spending endless hours by himself, kicking a soccer ball, as well as reading books about people who lived adventurous lives—he would tell his classmates that he wished his life were like one of those books. It was from these books that he also learned English.

When Ruben was in the third grade, he recalls watching the Olympics on TV for the first time, and deciding then and there that he would someday be an Olympian. Four years later, when the Winter Games were in Sarajevo, Ruben was again glued to the television set. This time, he saw someone who would change his life forever. He saw a little guy, around five feet three inches tall and looking as if he didn't weigh much more than a hundred pounds soaking wet, with an indomitable competitive spirit. That little guy was Scott Hamilton, and he went on to win the gold medal in figure skating. Scott became a major inspiration for Ruben, not only because he was a gold medal Olympian, but because he was also a cancer survivor. Ruben remembers saying to himself, "If he can do it, so can I."

Although he had no prior experience in the sport, Ruben chose the luge as the Olympic event he would compete in. He had strong legs and the spirit he needed to learn a new sport. Whereas most luge athletes become involved in the sport by the age of eleven, Ruben didn't start training until he was twenty-one. But Ruben didn't let his late start hold him back; simply, he was determined to succeed. He developed the mindset of believing in himself, and then set out to achieve his goal.

"The luge is like being on a bar of soap going down an obstacle course at 85 miles per hour."

Ruben knew making the U.S. Olympic luge team would be next to impossible. So instead of giving up on his dream, he got creative: He decided instead to form the first-ever luge team from his native country, Argentina. Ruben firmly believes that what you can conceive and believe, you can achieve. And for the first time in his life, he believed in himself— he felt confident he could compete in this sport he had developed such a passion for. It was that focus and perseverance that led Ruben Gonzalez to represent Argentina in three Winter Olympic Games.

Although his team didn't win any medals, Ruben did achieve his life-long dream to compete in a sport many thought he was too old to even attempt. Ruben proved he could succeed by giving his all, and today he hopes his story will help to inspire other young Latino athletes to become future Olympians.

"Choosing your focus in life can help you determine the road map for getting you where you need to be."

5

Success Is within You

DICK GONZALES
Former Senior Vice President of Human Resources, Safeway, Inc.

Being successful takes a strong inner drive—the drive to go from picking watermelons to running a grocery chain.

Dick Gonzales was born in Rocky Ford, Colorado, a small agricultural community famous for its cantaloupe and watermelon crops. In his early adulthood, he worked on ranches and in coal mines, and eventually landed a job packing watermelons. The migrant workers he worked around did most of the farming and harvesting, and rarely complained, even though their days were long and their work was hard and poorly paid.

Growing up in this type of environment made Dick realize at an early age that he had to work hard and pay his dues if he wanted to succeed. In Rocky Ford, most people viewed Latinos primarily as day laborers. Determined to never let such misconceptions deter him, Dick decided to make a difference, not just for himself but for the Hispanic community at large.

"Early in life, fuel your passion with dreams, and continue to refuel them as you continue to learn."

Dick strove to work smarter and to learn new skills. A born leader, Dick remembers working hard as a young man, but always knowing that one day he would be a person of importance. In fact, he believes that people should learn when they're young to lead by example, that it is during that time of their lives, as they are growing and beginning to take on responsibility, that learning how to lead will set them up for success. These lessons, Dick says, don't end once young men and women become adults. They should continue to learn throughout their lives, Dick says, because the mind is precious and we all should cherish our natural ability to think and be challenged.

Dick's first step up from working in the fields was when he learned the skill of plastering. In time, plastering became not only his trade but also his first small business. As a business owner, he learned valuable lessons about hard work and entrepreneurship, and realized that success is found within the individual. From this realization emerged his business mind-set: Dick had begun to think like an entrepreneur.

Dick also credits his success to the strong work ethic his father instilled in him, from as early as he can remember. His father taught him the importance of making sacrifices in life; how to work with others, as a team; and to never allow one's own interests to result in selfish behaviors or attitudes at work. Dick's mother was also a motivating influence, urging her son to aim for the top. She encouraged all her children to always strive to outperform the competition and to believe in their potential to succeed in life. She told them, "Never allow others to put you down and make you become stagnant. Instead, use it to your advantage; overcome the small roadblocks, and move forward."

"Reflect on your goals often, and with an eye toward growth."

Dick's mother also reminded him to take time to dream and focus on his goals. She always pushed her children to do better in school, and to keep an eye on the big picture—a college education. Dick says his mother always took an interest in her children's lives. "As you continue to grow," she would say, "always remember to remove as many barriers as possible and work hard toward accomplishing your goals." Knowing he had his parents' support helped Dick to focus his energy, on his path to success.

Dick envisioned becoming a person of importance, and set his mind to do whatever it took to become one. He served in the 25th Infantry Division of the U.S. Army in Vietnam, and later went on to college, where he had to work hard to support himself. The experiences he had in the Army and at college taught him leadership skills, as well as focus and discipline, two tools that would later prove invaluable to him as he worked his way up in the food retail industry.

"Dig within yourself and thrive."

Dick overcame adversity to become one of the few minorities to work his way to the executive ranks. He says he felt he had to work twice as hard as his nonminority competitors to reach the top. His desire and motivation, and the lessons his parents taught him about overcoming adversity and obstacles, also inspired him to ensure equal opportunities for the employees he managed. As his mother never let him forget, the United States is a multicultural and multinational economy, and it was important that Dick do more than remember where he came from—he had to believe in his Latino heritage.

6

Respect All People

BILL RICHARDSON
Governor of New Mexico

Success begins with respect: earn respect first by giving all people,
regardless of color, creed, or value system the respect they deserve.
People you respect will support your success.

Growing up familiar with two cultures—that of Mexico and the United States—is what Bill Richardson cherishes most about his heritage. Richardson is a comfortable member of both. Richardson was born in Pasadena, California, the son of an American banker and a Mexican secretary. He feels he is living the best of both worlds, thanks to growing up influenced by the rich culture of his mother at the same time he belonged to the diverse American way of life. His father was very proud of his American son, and his mother was equally proud of her Mexican son. This sense of pride was passed down to Bill, who claims the language and culture of both the United States and Mexico as his own. Growing up in the Richardson household, it was considered important that Bill be bilingual, so he learned to speak English from his father and Spanish from his mother.

"The best of both worlds is to have a Mexican and an American heritage."

Bill's parents always believed that their son could be whatever he chose to be in life, and instilled that belief in him early. Ultimately, this led him to earn his BA degree from Tufts University and his MA degree from Tufts' Fletcher School of Law and Diplomacy. In 2003, Bill Richardson became governor of New Mexico, elected by the widest margin of any candidate since 1964. Since then, Governor Richardson has become a major force in New Mexico, with a strong focus on issues meaningful to his constituents—such as helping to strengthen families by improving education, cutting taxes, and building a high-wage economy. In short, Richardson has built a career of acting in the best interests of the people.

Prior to becoming the governor of New Mexico, Richardson enjoyed a fulfilling career in public service, teaching at Harvard's Kennedy School of Government. In 1997, Richardson was nominated as the U.S. ambassador to the United Nations. In his role as ambassador, Richardson formed a vision of how best to address international negotiation challenges and crises throughout the world. He has met with powerful leaders throughout the world, negotiated the release of prisoners from the regime of Saddam Hussein, and has convinced foreign heads of state to step down. Richardson also has fought to increase the awareness of the status of women in Afghanistan and in Africa. He has been nominated four times for the Nobel Peace Prize in recognition of his worldwide humanitarian efforts throughout the years.

"A great and fulfilling life makes you feel good about living."

Governor Richardson's most recent political endeavor was to announce his candidacy for the U.S. presidency in 2008. And though he subsequently quit the race, it's clear that nothing is impossible for this great leader.

7

Focus, Teach, and Learn

Dr. Jerry Porras
Professor Emeritus, Stanford University

*Focusing on education is a crucial part of the foundation
of a strong Latino future.*

Imagine walking into Stanford University, a student pursuing an MBA from a top-tier program at one of the most prestigious universities in the world, and learning that one of the most reputable professors in the MBA program is Mexican–American. Would that change your opinion of that program? At Stanford University, Dr. Jerry Porras is one of Stanford University's chaired professors, and is known throughout the world as a Lane Professor of Organizational Behavior and Change.

Growing up in El Paso, Texas, Jerry "just knew" that he was bound to attend college, because his parents always emphasized the value of an education. With a little determination and very supportive parents, Jerry received his bachelor's degree in electrical engineering from Texas Western College (now the University of Texas at El Paso). At the time Jerry was a student there, he was one of few Latinos.

He vividly remembers walking down the aisle of the auditorium at his graduation ceremony, and thinking it was the last time he would see the inside of a university. But after working for a couple of years as an engineer, Jerry decided to pursue his MBA from Cornell University, and later received his PhD from the University of California, Los Angeles. Now called Dr. Porras, Jerry accepted a job in academia. As a professor, he has taught courses in leadership, interpersonal dynamics, and organizational development and change in MBA and executive leadership programs. And for sixteen years, he has directed Stanford Business School's Executive Program on Leading and Managing Change.

Dr. Porras attributes his success to hard work and, of course, a good education. An expert on organizational change, he has helped numerous clients in the United States, Mexico, and Argentina improve their organizational performance. And as a lecturer on visionary companies, he has delivered presentations to more than two hundred senior management audiences worldwide.

Dr. Porras also has served on the editorial boards of many academic publications, including the *Academy of Management Review, Business Review*, and the *Journal of Organizational Change Management*. He has written some forty articles or reviews and has published two books on organizational success. One of those books, *Stream Analysis: A Powerful New Way to Diagnose and Manage Organizational Change* (Prentice Hall, 1987), served as the basis for a widely used software tool for corporate structural redevelopment. With Jim Collins, Dr. Porras subsequently coauthored the international bestseller, *Built to Last: Successful Habits of Visionary Companies* (HarperCollins 1994). *Built to Last* is based on the results of an exhaustive six-year research project aimed at discovering the approaches and behaviors of the most visionary companies of the past two centuries.

In recognition of Dr. Porras's hard work and many successes, on September 3, 2007, *Hispanic Business* magazine editor and publisher, Jesus Chavaria, announced that Dr. Jerry Porras would receive the Lifetime Achievement Award at the magazine's annual Entrepreneur of the Year (EOY) Awards gala. The EOY honors the top Hispanic entrepreneurs of the year.

"The key is to pursue a solid education and establish a strong network."

Over the years, Dr. Porras has seen few representative Latino students, and even fewer in academia, corporate boardrooms, or senior-level management positions. He is a firm believer that the way to earn such positions is by first obtaining a solid education. Add to that a will to succeed and being part of a strong network, and you have a recipe for success, he says.

8

Success, Built One Venture at a Time

EDUARDO RALLO
Entrepreneur; Director and COO, Portfolio Management, Pacific Community Ventures

Serving the Latino demographic is a life mission.

Eduardo Rallo, who hails from Cuernavaca, Mexico, knew early in life that he wanted to be an entrepreneur. As a young man, inspired by the passion and the craft that Steven Spielberg exhibits in his movies, Eduardo started to think seriously of becoming a film director. Upon coming to the United States, he set his sights on going to college, first receiving a bachelor of arts degree in economics from the University of California at San Diego, and then an MBA from Harvard University.

Eduardo now serves as chief operating officer and director of Portfolio Management at Pacific Community Ventures (PCV). He is responsible for assuming seats on finance company boards, helping to recruit key management team members for portfolio companies, assisting in problem solving with portfolio company leaders, helping to develop new PCV initiatives with regard to service delivery, and working with the rest of the portfolio team through the due diligence and investment processes. That's his job, but Eduardo's passion is to empower the Latino community.

"The Latino demographic is one of the most underserved communities out there."

Prior to joining PCV, Eduardo cofounded World Wrapps, Inc., in 1994, where he served as vice president of store development until 1999. He also cofounded Brainstorm Ventures, a seed and early-stage technology fund that invested in twenty-four companies in the software, enabling technologies, infrastructure, and e-commerce fields. As managing partner, Eduardo served in an acting management, advisory, and/or board member role in several high-growth startups.

Bankers have long emulated the retail industry's marketing and distribution savvy. Now retailers are taking a page from the banker's playbook and reaching out to Latinos and their growing purchasing power. A recent report by the Food Marketing Institute found that, in 2004, Latino families in the United States had purchasing power in the amount of $686 billion, a figure expected to reach $1 trillion by 2010.

"The Latino demographic is one of the most underserved communities out there," says Eduardo, who is also founder and chairman of Farmacia Remedios, a startup pharmacy chain that caters to the [Latino] community. The growing Latino population and its particular needs make this market irresistible, Eduardo says, noting that language barriers alone make misdiagnosis and incorrect prescriptions a serious problem for this population. "There might be two hundred options in a Walgreens aisle, but you don't really know which one to choose if you do not speak the language," he adds. Farmacia Remedios offers pharmacy products with bilingual labels, enabling members of the Latino community who do not speak English to understand what they are buying.

"The sky's the limit for the Latino market."

In addition to being a savvy entrepreneur, Eduardo is reaching out to help serve the community from which he came. In this way he serves as an example to others, both in business and the public at large.

II

UNITY

Think about working toward a goal and needing help along the way but not having anyone around to help you. Then think about reaching your goals but having no one around to celebrate your success with you. There is a saying, "If you want to get somewhere fast, go alone. But if you want to travel far, go together." If your goal is to reach for the top, keep in mind you cannot do it alone. And whatever your goal, know that there is a network of people who can support you. People who try to do things alone will fail in the long term. Even athletes in individual sports have a support system, made up of coaches, trainers, agents, fans, and friends and family.

To strengthen your goals and set yourself up for success, you need to reach out to individuals in your community who believe in the same things you do; you need to seek power and support from those around you. By building a network in support of your goals, you create a link between them and those of your peers and/or community. Put another way, to empower your goals, share them with others.

Working within a community toward a common goal allows for collaboration, making it easier to build on ideas and achieve your objectives. The individuals whose stories we feature in this section demonstrate a strong sense of unity, whether in the form of a network, sports team, or community. For most of them, however, unity began with family. Cross-culturally, one of the most important character-building elements is a strong family foundation.

To be successful, we must work toward completing one another, not competing with each other.

9

Build on Your Community

HENRY CISNEROS
Chairman and CEO, American City Vista

Keep in mind the people you are serving—how is this focus going to help or hinder them? Don't ever give up because people say you can't or shouldn't.

The dream of becoming the first Latino to serve as mayor of a major U.S. city became a reality for Henry Cisneros early in his career when, in 1981, he took that office in San Antonio, Texas. His election was well deserved, as Cisneros had always taken a sincere interest in helping the general public through local government. Serving the public, he demonstrated, gives a person leverage, specifically by understanding the business community and helping the people in the surrounding neighborhoods.

Cisneros served four terms in the mayor's office. During those years, he helped rebuild the city's economic base and created jobs through massive infrastructure improvements and restructuring the downtown area—earning San Antonio the reputation as one of the most progressive cities of that era. In recognition of his achievements, in 1984, Cisneros was considered for the Democratic vice presidential nomination; in 1986, *City and State Magazine* gave him its Outstanding Mayor in the Nation Award.

Cisneros' career path led him next to take on the role of Secretary of the U.S. Department of Housing and Urban Development in President Bill Clinton's cabinet, from 1993 to 1996.

With his determination and a focus on building the community, Cisneros has been credited with initiating a major revitalization of many of the nation's public housing developments, as well as formulating policies that have contributed to today's improved homeownership rate. His goal is to build new homes in urban areas, and to create affordable homeownership programs for urban families. In this effort, Cisneros has helped his constituents understand that the key principle to homeownership is realizing that renting need not be a lifetime choice, but rather a transition toward owning a home.

Using his background in urban planning and politics, Cisneros also founded American City Vista, an organization whose twofold mission is to make affordable homes available to first-time buyers and to forge stronger ties among the people of the Latino community.

"Revitalizing your community brings pride."

It is Henry Cisneros' respect for the community he grew up in that led to the emergence of America City Vista, which is responsible for revitalizing neighborhoods in Denver, Colorado and for building affordable homes in central areas of Austin, Texas, and Los Angeles, California. Similar plans are underway in Houston, Texas, in the near future. The organization is also focused on creating a significant number of "villages within a city"—homes built in metropolitan areas—that bring new life to neighborhoods.

"The key to home ownership is to visualize driving to your own home, up your own driveway, and into your own garage."

Cisneros' philosophy is that building in the community begins when individuals reach out to likeminded others—simply put, the more people pitch in and work as a team, the better off everyone will be.

10

Build the Community through Empowerment

RAUL YZAGUIRRE
Former President of the National Council of La Raza

Use a compass to identify Latino leaders in your community.

Born in the Rio Grande Valley of South Texas, Raul Yzaguirre began his civil rights career at 15, when he organized a junior auxiliary chapter of a Hispanic veteran's organization.

Yzaguirre is the former president of the National Council of La Raza (NCLR), the largest constituency-based national Hispanic organization and leading Hispanic think tank in America. After four years in the U.S. Air Force Medical Corps, he founded the National Organization for Mexican American Services (NOMAS). It was a proposal he wrote for NOMAS that led to the creation of what is now NCLR.

Yzaguirre joined NCLR in 1974 and has spearheaded its emergence as the country's most influential and respected advocate for Hispanics. In the process, he has become known as an unrelenting leader for *la causa* (the cause), whose mission is to address a twofold problem: first, the Latino community at large is not unified, and there is no vehicle in place to drive that unity; second, the Latino community does not have institutions that are programmatic in nature. There are, of course wonderful institutions in the Latino community, such as the American GI Forum, but they do not have the capability to deal with the problem of social injustice. Most of these institutions are volunteer-based and, as such, are not professionally run or strategically placed, with an established timeline for accomplishing goals.

"It is important in life to believe in something that will give you satisfaction."

Yzaguirre remembers being frustrated by the lack of avenues for action, so he conceived a regional organization and submitted a proposal to the Ford Foundation, asking for funding to launch it. Although the vice president of the Ford Foundation turned him down at the time, Yzaguirre assured him, "I won't ignore what you have brought to my attention; I will do something about it." Yzaguirre kept his word: he went on and found three people he empowered to start the Southwest Council of La Raza. He reached out to Dr. Ernesto Galarza, a PhD from Harvard, who had been a farmworker organizer and an educator; Dr. Julian Samora, a sociologist from Notre Dame; and Herman Gallegos, a social worker and community organizer.

Through his work, Yzaguirre has become the Latino community's enduring civil rights pioneer, its compass, and its conscience. At the Washington, DC-based NCLR, he articulates the agenda for more than 40 million Hispanics. Throughout his 30 years as president of the NCLR, Yzaguirre helped build the organization into the largest Latino civil rights and advocacy organization in the country. With affiliates in 41 states, the NCLR serves millions of Hispanics across the country and works to expand opportunities for all Americans through education, advocacy, and lobbying. His work for the advancement of Latinos has been invaluable— all in the name of community. In recognition of his great achievements, in 2005, the organization's headquarters building in Washington, DC, was named after him.

Yzaguirre has been honored on many occasions for his work: He was the first Hispanic to receive a Rockefeller Public Service Award from Princeton University, and he received the Order of the Aztec Eagle, the highest honor given by the government of Mexico to noncitizens.

At the time of this writing, Yzaguirre was serving as a national co-chair of Hillary Clinton's presidential campaign, and as chair of her Hispanic outreach effort. "Hillary Clinton has spent more than three decades advocating on behalf of those who are invisible in America," Yzaguirre says. "[She] has the ability to bring people together to get results and move this country forward."

11

Bridge the Corporate Gap

CARLOS ORTA
President and CEO, Hispanic Association for Corporate Responsibility

Identify Latino talent to work in Fortune 500 companies and increase the visibility of your true passion in the private sector.

Carlos Orta has made a career of helping his community. For the past 18 years, wherever he has lived, he has made it his mission to become involved in various volunteer efforts and to serve on numerous boards, panels, and committees for community-based organizations, locally, regionally, and nationally. Currently, Orta participates as board member of Padres Contra El Cancer in Los Angeles, California. He has also served on the board of directors of the Kansas City Hispanic Chamber of Commerce, and led the efforts that established the Hispanic Business Political Action Committee of Greater Kansas City. In Missouri, he was a board member of the Missouri State Chamber of Commerce, and coauthored the executive order that created the Missouri Governor's Commission on Hispanic Affairs. In Miami, he served as chairman of Leadership Miami, and was on the board of directors of the Young Leaders Society (United Way of Miami), Hands on Miami, and Kids Voting (Miami–Dade County Chapter). He was also the board of Big Brothers and Big Sisters, where, for two years, he also functioned as a big brother.

Orta is also very busy as the president and CEO of the Hispanic Association for Corporate Responsibility (HACR), a national organization that helps to address the lack of Latino representation in corporate America. To that end, it identifies members of this population who are qualified to work in Fortune 500 companies. In this effort, HACR partners with a 14-member board of national grass-roots organizations committed to increasing Hispanic representation among executives and in other positions in Fortune 500 companies. The group, in partnership with the Harvard Business School, has created the Corporate Governance program as a way to address the issue. The class of 2007 brought the number of alumni available to serve on corporate boards to 150.

"America is beginning to witness Hispanics become members of the elite class in Fortune 500 companies."

Next on the HACR agenda is to obtain commitments from corporations interested in the Hispanic consumer market to ensure that their boardrooms—and policymaking executives—mirror their changing customer base. HACR will then invite the corporations to increase the number of Hispanics serving on U.S. corporate boards.

Already, the list of HACR corporate members continues to grow, underscoring the importance of the organization's mission to increase the participation of the community in all aspects of corporate operations—employment, procurement, philanthropy, and governance.

In September 2004, prior to joining HACR, Orta joined Anheuser-Busch, Inc. as director of community outreach for the western region. There he was responsible for the company's Latino community outreach efforts, which included developing and maintaining relationships with new and emerging community leaders; directing corporate, philanthropic, and media-related contributions throughout the region; and recommending funding levels for local and regional community-based organizations.

12

Bring the Network Together

DONNA BLANCERO, PhD

Director and Associate Professor, Touro International University College of Business

Set high standards for yourself and others, and for working together as a team, foundation, background, and education.

Growing up in Brooklyn, New York taught Donna Blancero lessons in understanding diverse cultures. She grew up in a blue-collar, working-class neighborhood, home to many different ethnic groups. On one block, she saw Jewish, African-American, and Latino families living together, side by side.

Her father, who pumped gas for a living, always stressed the importance of getting good grades and completing school so that she wouldn't have to do his kind of work. With her father's encouragement, Donna began early to set high expectations for herself. The youngest in her family, she became the only one to obtain a college education.

"Set high standards to get ahead."

Blancero received her bachelor of science degree from the State University of New York (SUNY) at Old Westbury, a master of science degree in Human Resources Management from the New York Institute of Technology, and a doctorate in industrial relations from Cornell University.

Both Blancero's parents taught her to be proud of her Puerto Rican heritage and, at the same time, to treat all people with respect, regardless of their ethnicity. She was very sensitive to injustices of this nature, for her father had a thick Spanish accent, and encountered a fair amount of discrimination as result. She recalls inviting her high school friends to her house one day, and them not being able to understand her father when he spoke to them in English—they assumed he was speaking Spanish. They told Donna, "We're sorry, we don't speak Spanish." In disbelief, Donna explained to them that it was English he was speaking. The friends replied with a simple, "Oh!" Donna never forgot that experience, or the neighborhood where she grew up.

Suffering herself from the absence of mentors in her neighborhood as a child, Blancero today believes they are essential to helping kids in lower-income neighborhoods achieve academic success. She stresses that Latino youth need to be connected to professionals who are willing to spend time with them, otherwise many of these children will become discouraged by the negative perceptions others have of them, and never develop the confidence they need to progress in school. With the right guidance, she believes, it's only a matter of time before they will realize they have what it takes to be successful.

"Bring the network together and choose the right mentor."

Dr. Blancero spent many years as a professor at Arizona State University (ASU), where she would proudly introduce herself on the first day of class each semester as a Latina from Brooklyn. She wanted both her Latino and Latina students to become aware immediately that they, too, could succeed in academia. As one of a very few Latino faculty members at ASU's Business School, Dr. Blancero came to see that to increase the number of Latino students in college and, later, in corporate boardrooms, education must be supplemented by networking and mentoring. Simply, to move up the ladder in corporate America, it's critical to know the right people.

Dr. Blancero feels that the doctorate program at ASU has the right vision: to put people of all races in front of the classroom. When all ethnicities are represented at the highest levels of academia, it becomes widely accepted that people of all backgrounds are capable of achieving the greatest goals in college. Today, as director and associate dean at Touro University International College of Business, she has implemented her teaching philosophy and style from ASU to Touro University.

Donna believes that mentoring today's youth is a vital element to help prepare them for the future. It is important to encourage Latino youth to seek a college education so that they can compete in today's business environment. Therefore, one of the most important things young professionals can do, Blancero says, is to encourage other young Latinos in the country to pursue academic careers. If you have a few hours to spare and are a Latino college graduate, you can make a significant contribution to your community by becoming a mentor.

13

Move Out of Your Comfort Zone

DOUGLAS PATINO
Philanthropist and Community Leader

Education is a key tool for climbing the ladder of success.

If Douglas Patino had his way, every Latino and Latina in the United States would become a college graduate. In addition to his community work and significant contributions to the economy though his work in government, Dr. Patino has made a career of helping young Latinos make their college dreams come true, and has led an extraordinary life in the process.

"Having an education is one of the key pillars for living a successful life in the United States."

In the Latino community, Dr. Patino is known as one of the nation's leading philanthropists, and in the California State University system as a successful former vice chancellor emeritus. He has, simply, touched the lives of countless Latinos who have benefited from his charitable work and tireless efforts to improve their educational prospects.

Dr. Patino credits his humble upbringing and his mother's generous nature as instrumental in becoming the person he is today. His family was poor, yes, but, he says, his mother always opened the door of their home to friends and family in need. Thus, as a youngster, Douglas learned that taking care of those less fortunate was a way of life.

He attended school in Mexicali, Mexico until the third grade, which he remembers as resembling the school on the television series *Little House on the Prairie*. He spent the remainder of his early school years in Calexico, California, which borders Mexicali.

Patino's family taught him to work hard, in school and at jobs he held, no matter how undesirable they might be. So even when scrubbing toilets, Patino did the work with integrity. During his high school years, he worked at a local drugstore, where he learned to be responsible at a young age. After high school, he received an associate of arts degree from Imperial Valley College, and went on to earn his bachelor's degree in political science from San Diego State University.

Douglas continued his academic career, obtaining a master of arts degree in counseling from San Diego State University. And later, he was fortunate to have a mentor who provided him with the resources to follow his dream of obtaining a doctorate in human behavior development, which he received from the United States International University at San Diego.

Ever since, Patino has worked with Latinos in his community, in one way or another. In his mid-twenties, despite being an up-and-comer in the California state capital, he left his post to help a community group raise money in Sacramento. He was proud of making a difference and wanted to do more, so a few years later, he took a job with former governor Jerry Brown as a department director, a position that allowed him to help fund programs in the community. After his appointment ended, Patino started a nonprofit foundation that enabled him to continue to aid the community. Dr. Patino believes that college is the foundation all Latinos need to follow their dreams and have successful careers. (Notably, all ten of the Patino children received a college education.) But he also acknowledges the challenge to making this a reality, for his research has revealed that most Latino children begin to lose interest in school around the fifth or sixth grade. Mentors, he says, are needed to help keep children on the right academic track. He points out that though California is one of the wealthiest states in the country, and one of the places with the most resources in the world, it resembles a third-world country in that political seats are rarely held by Latinos/Latinas. Without a political voice, the needs of the Latino community cannot be met adequately.

Dr. Patino believes that Latinos can learn from the successes of the African-American community, which has faced, and continues to face, similar struggles. The people of the Latino community must learn to work together to empower each other today and in the future. Dr. Patino believes it's time for Latinos to move out of their comfort zone and find ways to remove the barriers that exist in their communities. He also believes that they have to become clear about their purpose and the contribution they want to make in life. He stresses that people are not defined by the jobs they have, but by the impact they make. What is important, and what defines leadership, he says, is the passion each of us has inside.

14

Give to the Fullest

Janet Murguia
President and CEO, National Council of La Raza; Executive Producer, Alma Awards

Dream big, and strive to become a leader.

Janet Murguia has emerged as one of the new civil rights leaders in the Latino community. Since January 1, 2005, she has served as the president and CEO of the National Council of La Raza (NCLR), the largest national civil rights and advocacy organization for Hispanics in the United States. The focus of the NCLR is to improve opportunities for Hispanic Americans through its network of nearly three hundred affiliated community-based organizations.

Before joining the NCLR, Murguia spent several years in Washington, DC, where she began her career in the political arena as a legislative counsel to former Kansas congressman Jim Slattery. Later, she was former President Clinton's deputy assistant, where her job was to provide the president with strategic and legislative advice on key issues affecting our country. She also served as deputy director of legislative affairs, managing the legislative staff and acting as a senior White House liaison to Congress. Later, Murguia had the unique opportunity to serve as campaign manager for the 2000 Gore/Lieberman presidential campaign.

After graduating from the University of Kansas, Murguia returned there in 2001 as executive chancellor of university relations, where she was able to build programs at the university. With her powerful voice in the Latino community, and her dedication to improving the lives of

Latinos through her leadership at the NCLR, she has earned the respect and recognition of many organizations in the United States. In 2007, she was named as one of *Poder* magazine's "The Poderosos 100," one of *Latino* Magazine's "101 Top Leaders in the Hispanic Community," and one of *Hispanic* magazine's "100 Most Influential Hispanics." In 2006, Murguia was included among *Washington* magazine's "100 Most Powerful Women in Washington" and *People En Español*'s "100 Most Influential Hispanics 2006." And, in 2005, she was a finalist in *Hispanic* magazine's "Woman of the Year" award.

"Striving to be the very best is within all of us. It is important to never give up."

Janet grew up in Kansas City, Kansas, in the Argentine district, which she remembers as a vibrant community made up of immigrants, mainly from Mexico, many of whom worked for the Santa Fe Railroad or in silver mining. Her parents, Mexican immigrants, had only fifth- and seventh-grade educations, but never failed to instill in their children the value of education. Janet's father worked hard in a steel plant, while her mother provided day care for the neighborhood children.

The inspiration provided by her parents led Janet to do well in school and to go on to obtain both a bachelor's degree in journalism and Spanish, and a juris doctor degree from the University of Kansas. Her parents have much to be proud of, for in addition to Janet, their other children have succeeded in their careers, as well. Janet's brother, Carlos, and sister, Mary, are the first-ever Latino brother and sister to both be confirmed by the U.S. Senate as Federal Court judges. Janet's other brother, Ramon, obtained a law degree from Harvard University. Thus, the Murguia family serves as an inspiration to all Latino families, proving that *si se puede* (it is possible) to live the American dream— to get a good education and achieve success in life. They also serve as role models through the wonderful work they do in the Hispanic community.

Janet Murguia continues to encourage Latinos to dream big and to aspire to high levels of success and leadership. She is proud to see that Latinos today are having a major impact in American society by becoming entrepreneurs and by gaining political clout. In 2008, it is expected that 2.5 million Latinos will vote in the presidential election. Janet is also proud to be the executive producer of the Alma Awards, a program that showcases Latino talent.

15

Build Your Empire Together, Rather Than Alone

DAVID LIZARRAGA
Chairman, President, CEO, The East Los Angeles Community Union

The building of an empire begins in one's own backyard.

Every community in the United States has characteristics that reflect the heart of its individual members. Building an empire starts in the community. You have to believe in the endeavor, be patient, and start small; good things will happen.

So believes David Lizarraga, who was born and raised in East Los Angeles, California. As a young man there he began working with young at-risk teens and their families, to give the economically disadvantaged access to tools and resources to pursue the American dream.

"Filling empty buildings in Latino neighborhoods brings in life."

Growing up in LA in the 1960s, David recalls seeing the city plunged into a devastating economic decline, scarring the face of the community with boarded-up businesses and discarded factories. In this decade marked by desperation, David saw businesses abandoned by major companies, companies the community had helped build over generations. But the human toll, he says, was even greater.

Witnessing such devastation as a young man gave David compassion for the people left behind and drove him to dream about how to fill those empty buildings again. It was the imminent threat to the spirit of the neighborhood that brought together a group of community leaders, who formed The East Los Angeles Community Union (TELACU), dedicated to getting people involved and lending a helping hand.

Thus, TELACU was born out of the deep desire of the community at large to improve the lives of its citizens. The challenge was monumental, recalls David, but TELACU's members were driven by passion, to "provide people with the tools for self-empowerment and self-sufficiency, and with the opportunities to use those tools to improve lives."

In the end, David Lizarraga's vision of transforming abandoned buildings into viable businesses became a reality. The necessary capital and funding were raised to help rebuild and revitalize the community, creating jobs and offering opportunities to the needy community. Once their community was revitalized, and jobs again became available, families could begin to build nest eggs, to secure the future of their children.

Over time, TELACU became one of the largest and the most successful community development corporations in the nation. It was David's business savvy and hands-on involvement that empowered both his community and the union. As a result, today, he is regarded internationally as one of the country's top Latino leaders. He was past chairman of the board of the United States Hispanic Chamber of Commerce, and he is CEO of TELACU, where he establishes partnerships to meet his objective of helping Latinos succeed in business.

David also has been instrumental in developing quality housing for thousands of low-income senior citizens throughout southern California. He is dedicated to achieving his goals to improve the Latino community by empowering families and entrepreneurs and encouraging parents to establish an education foundation to send their children to college. He also encourages small business owners to join their local chamber of commerce, so they become involved with the greater business community.

"Nobody does it alone. We need to build unity together."

16

Think with the Heart

ALCARIO AND CARMEN CASTELLANO
Founders, Castellano Family Foundation

Believe in destiny, and always open your heart to new opportunities.

One day in 2001, Alcario Castellano walked into a local store in his Cambrian neighborhood in San Jose, California, and bought a $10.00 lottery ticket. Early the next morning, coffee in hand, Al checked the winning lotto numbers in the newspaper. He pulled out his ticket and read each number, one by one, comparing them to those on his ticket. Impossible as it was to believe, Al realized he was staring at the winning ticket, worth $141 million. He checked the numbers, again and again. Still somewhat in shock, he went for a walk to clear his head, and to decide how he was going to tell his wife Carmen they had become millionaires overnight.

"Choose a lifelong partner who has dreams."

Al was born in Artesia, New Mexico, and had grown up poor. When he was nine years old, the family moved to California, where at a young age, he learned the value of hard work—he picked cotton in the San Joaquin Valley, harvested garlic and apricots, and picked plums. Later the family settled in Hollister, California.

While attending high school, Al worked evenings and weekends as a grocery clerk. Upon graduation, he joined the U.S. Army and served two years, primarily in the San Francisco Bay Area. He went on to work in the aerospace industry in the Bay Area until 1970, when he became a retail clerk at a supermarket, until his retirement in 1990.

Carmen was born in Watsonville, California, where her father owned a trucking business, and her mother owned a Mexican meat market in Pajaro, California. Thanks to the example of her parents, Carmen learned entrepreneurial skills early in life. She later attended Heald Business College in San Jose, where she completed an executive secretary program.

"Destiny is on my side."

Needless to say, winning $141 million dollars caused Al and Carmen to think long and hard what they would do with their newfound wealth. Rather than squander it, as so many lottery winners do, they chose to start the Castellano Family Foundation, with the mission of cultivating the enrichment of Latino family values through the support of organizations, primarily in the Santa Clara County community in California.

"Cultivate the enrichment of Latino family values."

Carmen is president of the foundation, whose primary focus is to promote Latino arts, culture, and leadership, and to encourage the educational pursuits of Latino students. As of June 30, 2005, the Castellano Family Foundation has awarded grants to more than 60 organizations, totaling $1,400,000.

The work and generosity of the Castellanos has not gone unnoticed in the community. In 2002, they were honored to receive the Portraits of

Success Award for their exemplary leadership in the Latino community. In May 2004, they received an ABBY award, given by the Arts Council in Silicon Valley, for their community leadership and support of the arts. And in May 2006, Al and Carmen received the Distinguished Philanthropist of the Year Award from the Latino Community Foundation.

"Giving back is key."

17

Succeed Together

DR. FRANCES MORALES
Assistant Dean of Students, and Director of El Centro Chicano, Stanford University

*Working to improve the education of migrant students and their families
is an empowering experience.*

Dr. Frances Morales well remembers the first words that influenced her. They were two English words: yes and no. She was told that the difference between them meant the difference between being deported to Mexico and staying in the United States. Frances was about five years old when she recalls her play time being interrupted by two tall men dressed in green, wearing pistols at their sides. "Are you a U.S. citizen?" they asked her. Luckily, her sister and brother had drilled her on how to answer the question: "If the border patrol asks you if you are a U.S. citizen, answer yes."

It was not always easy to be brave, Frances says, especially when an undocumented aunt was staying with them, and border patrol officers were searching outside and threatening to come inside. Hiding with her aunt and cousins in a closet, Frances prayed fervently that her infant cousin would not let out a cry and give away their hiding place.

When Frances started kindergarten, she thought school would be fun, that it would be a place to learn and make friends. It was anything but, for she soon learned she would need to know much more than how to say yes and no in English. She had not been given any rehearsed answers for the questions the nuns asked her. So she would take a chance, responding yes to some questions and no to others. She fooled no one, and was eventually placed in the front row, where it was thought she would learn more quickly. But she didn't like the front row, and being there didn't help her to understand the nun's instructions any better. Frances would almost always receive a big, fat, red zero on her papers. And if Frances tried to ask another student sitting near her whether she had done her work correctly, the nun would take Frances to the closet, pull up her skirt, and spank her with the ruler.

Finally, things began to change for Frances in the third grade, when a kind and patient nun took an interest in Frances. This nun looked for ways to motivate Frances, which made her feel good, and part of the class. Soon she was enjoying school and getting good grades. She really shone when people believed in her and expected her to succeed, rather than automatically assuming she would fail.

"Do unto others as you would have them do unto you."

Frances enrolled in public school in the ninth grade, where for the first time she experienced segregation—Latinos were taught separately from the Caucasian students. Frances' Spanish teacher, Mrs. Carrizales, was one of only two Mexican teachers at Mary Hoge Junior High, and she spoke openly with her students about things she heard in the teachers' lounge—such as, "Why should [Mexican students] take college prep classes if they are just going to be field workers and maids?" Mrs. Carrizales was determined to teach her students that they would have to fight for themselves and for their education, and believe in themselves even when the counselors and other teachers did not.

Shortly after she finished ninth grade, Frances' family moved from Texas to Fresno, California, where she finished high school. After graduating, she was accepted into the California Mini-Corps program, in which college students served as teachers' assistants in schools for migrant children. Being with so many first-generation college students working to improve the educational opportunities of migrants and their families was an empowering experience for Frances.

Frances then enrolled at California State University, Fresno (CSUF). After receiving her bachelor of arts degree in Spanish, she earned a multiple-subject teaching credential, and started working as a substitute teacher in Fresno. Her desire to provide better educational opportunities and counseling to Chicano/Mexican American students inspired her to pursue a master's degree in guidance and counseling at the University of New Mexico in Albuquerque.

She returned to CSUF, now holding the title of assistant coordinator of advising services and coordinator of tutorial services. After a year there, she began the doctoral program in curriculum and teacher education, with an emphasis on bilingual education at Stanford University. This opened the door to her conducting research on effective teaching practices and bilingual programs.

Today, Frances is the assistant dean of students, and director of El Centro Chicano at Stanford University, where she mentors, advises, and encourages Latino students. It is a major undertaking, for Stanford University is committed to diversity: About 50 percent of the freshman classes are composed of students of color, with approximately 1,200 Chicano/Latino students; about 10 percent of the freshman class is Chicano/Latino, and about 25 percent of those students are first-generation college students.

El Centro Chicano serves as a hub for student leadership development for Chicano/Latino students. There are about 20 voluntary student organizations, ranging from community service to preprofessional and cultural groups and organizations. El Centro Chicano also organizes major cultural events, such as El Dia de los Muertos, Posadas, and holds a Cesar Chavez Commemoration. It also sponsors an annual Community Awards Program to acknowledge the academic, leadership, and community service contributions of students, along with the contributions of faculty, staff, and alumni.

"To whom much is given, much is expected."

III

TENACITY

To develop strength of character and drive yourself forward in life, you will need to be tenacious. Tenacity gives you resiliency and helps you maintain your course of action as you seek to achieve what you value or desire. Being tenacious means you do not give up on your goals and aspirations, even in the face of adversity. It means you have a dogged determination to recover from a setback, to adjust to change, and to meet challenges no matter how daunting they seem.

Being tenacious also means you believe in yourself, even when you fail, as everyone does on occasion. To be successful, you must view failures and setbacks as learning opportunities, and prevent them from dampening your spirit or eroding your self-esteem. Successful people know they must pick themselves up after they've been knocked down, dust themselves off, and, if need be, start all over again.

But to make it to the top, you will need more than tenacity; you must also have a plan of action (your focus), and then execute it—know where you are going, how you plan to get there, and what beacons to follow. Tenacity, coupled with a plan of action, will get you where you want to go.

18

Push on the Door Until You Get In

Richard Leza
Venture Capitalist, Chairman and CEO, AI Research

Never give up.

A door will open if you push on it long enough, Richard Leza's mother always told him. Others may want to keep it closed, but just keep up the pressure, she said, and sooner or later, they will get tired.

Richard Leza is born a leader who understands that pressure is part of life. The key, he says, is to focus on the big picture, and keep in mind that there will be a payoff down the road if you are persistent and apply your energy in the direction you want to go.

"Doors don't open easily. You have to push at them."

Richard's family included six brothers and three sisters, so money was always in short supply. They were raised in a traditional Mexican family, in the small town of Hatch, New Mexico, sixty miles north of El Paso, Texas. His *barrio* was primarily a farming community, where he could smell onions and strawberries growing, and see cotton fields in the distance. At his school, Hatch Valley High, the dropout rate was about 80 percent, with most of the kids leaving school to work in the fields.

Richard's first role models were his mother and *abuelo* (grandfather). His mother always expected her son to graduate from high school—she would accept no excuses for his not doing so. So he stayed in high school, but he had no plans to go on to college. He, too, worked in the fields, picking crops with the *braceros* (farmers). But he did more. As he worked in the hot, beating sun, Richard began to pay close attention to the treatment of his coworkers. He realized they were being unfairly paid and how that was happening. Eventually, he walked up to the *jefe* (boss) and challenged him, advocating on behalf of the *braceros*, mostly Spanish-speaking workers. He had worked out the numbers and could prove what he was saying. Richard's advocacy for these workers resulted in the braceros getting paid what they had earned.

As for himself, Richard turned out to be one of the best pickers, making 35 to 40 cents an hour. This hard labor gave him a valuable work ethic, which would stand him in good stead as he began determine his future. With his mother's encouragement, Richard decided he would go to college. Leaving behind most of his friends who continued working in the fields, he moved to Los Angeles to attend East Los Angeles College (ELAC). There he decided to major in computer technology. His mother's inspiration drove him to succeed. After he received his first degree, his AA in computer technology, he began working as a draftsman, making $3.50 per hour, ten times what he had earned doing hard labor in the fields.

After gaining experience in part-time computer jobs, he decided it was time to pursue a bachelor of science degree. He chose New Mexico State University (NMSU) as the place to achieve this academic goal. While at NMSU, Richard received devastating news. He was diagnosed with cancer, and was a given only a 10 percent chance to live. Fortunately, following surgery and chemotherapy treatment, it became clear he would be one of that lucky 10 percent.

Feeling blessed that he had regained his health, Richard once again began to think about the future. His first decision was to decide whether to go back to school. Now married, and with the support of his wife and mother, he came to the conclusion that giving up wasn't an option. Back to school he went, and after a few years, had earned his bachelor's degree in engineering.

Next Richard decided to apply to the top five business schools in the country, to enroll in an MBA program. He was somewhat put off when he got negative reactions from some of friends his friends and colleagues, especially when he told them his first choice was Stanford University. They pointed out how expensive it was, and the high scholastic requirements. They also emphasized that he was Mexican-American, and with NMSU as his undergrad school, warned him that Stanford was a long shot.

But he proved them all wrong. In 1978, he earned his MBA from Stanford, and later went on to receive an honorary doctor of law degree from NMSU. Twenty-eight years later, and with experience in many different fields—finance, manufacturing, engineering, and medical device software—and as an entrepreneur in numerous start-up companies, including Optimal learning Corporation, Endo Therapeutics Corporation, and CastalLink, Inc., he was ready to pursue his next dream: to work in a venture capital firm.

However, after approaching the partners of a number of firms, saying, "I have everything you need—experience and a good education," he came up empty. Richard began to feel that being Hispanic kept him from getting the jobs he wanted. Remembering his mother's words about closed doors, Richard decided to take another tack—he'd work on getting in through the back door. He started putting together deals for entrepreneurs and finding equity for them, and he got involved in projects that the venture firms weren't interested in.

"You must be persistent and follow your dreams."

Today, Richard is the chairman and chief executive officer of AI research Corporation in Mountain View, California, a venture capital firm specializing in high-technology start-ups. He is also the cofounder and past chairman of Hispanic-Net, a nonprofit organization dedicated to improving and enhancing entrepreneurial opportunities for Hispanics, and the author of two successful books: *Develop Your Business Plan*, and *Export Now: A Guide for Small Businesses*.

Richard also has established a fellowship for Hispanic students at the Stanford Graduate School of Business, and a scholarship for Hispanic engineering students at New Mexico State University. His achievements and acts of generosity were recognized by *Hispanic* magazine, when they named Richard one of America's 100 most influential Hispanics.

Richard continues to be a wonderful role model to many, but none more important than his son, Richard Jr., who has followed in his father's footsteps by earning an MBA from Stanford, in 1995. To this day, Richard attributes his great success to his wife, Cindy, and his mother. Without them, he says, he wouldn't be where he is today.

19

The Drive to Win

President, Sterling Hispanic Capital Group Division of Vfinance Investments

Believing in your convictions and pursuing your dreams will drive you to success.

Successful people are passionate about their dreams. They pursue those dreams with conviction, and their positive energy becomes contagious to those around them.

People aren't born knowing what they need to achieve success, Charles Patrick Garcia says; they acquire it. As a White House Fellow, working for Deputy Secretary of State John Whitehead in the Reagan administration, he remembers Whitehead teaching him that to get things done, you have to get out of your office. Thanks to Whitehead's wise mentorship, Charles learned how to focus on the process of government, to understand the interrelationships among the executive and judiciary branches, the press, special-interest groups, and the think tanks. He also developed savvy about Washington's bureaucracy, from top to bottom.

"Spread positive energy."

Charles had learned discipline as a young man, when he attended the U.S. Air Force Academy and, later, earned his law degree from Columbia University. His experiences and education put him on track to become a successful entrepreneur, which he achieved at age thirty-six, when he cofounded Sterling Financial Group, which today has grown to sixty offices in seven different countries. In 2000 and 2001, *Hispanic* magazine named his company one of the fastest-growing Hispanic-owned businesses. His leadership capabilities have also won him positions in the administration of three U.S. presidents.

Charles believes that to overcome adversity, you must learn to find solutions to your own problems. By doing, he says, you become tenacious, which will ultimately lead to triumphs for you.

"To overcome adversity, you must learn to find solutions to your own problems."

In his book, *A Message from Garcia* (John Wiley & Sons, Inc., 2003), Charles writes about believing in yourself and standing by your convictions. He tells how his first act of conviction was to refuse to follow the road map his father, a successful physician in Panama, had planned for him. He was determined to follow his own dreams. He stresses that the only person who can effectively push you is *you*. In high school, he joined the junior ROTC, and the Rangers program, in order to hone his leadership skills while still very young. After two years of Junior ROTC, his principal recommended that he apply to the Air Force Academy, one of the top, and toughest, schools in the United States

This he did, and entirely on his own—he was determined to pay his tuition himself, with scholarships. He recalls thinking that if he let his father do this for him, he would then have to answer to him about his performance.

By staying true to himself, Charles even won over his father, who told him how proud he was of his son. Shortly after graduation, Charles became a White House Fellow, and he never looked back, always pursuing his own dreams, with tenacity, passion, and conviction.

20

The Brooklyn Way

RAY SUAREZ
Senior News Correspondent, National Public Radio

Remember where you come from and where you are going.

Growing up, Ray Suarez had the ideal vista from which to view the Manhattan skyline—the elevated train platform in his Brooklyn neighborhood. Though his father, Rafael Sr. made great sacrifices, working 70 hours a week, so he could move his family to a better neighborhood—from Crown Heights to Bensonhurst to Flatbush—the new *barrio* was much like the old one. Endless rows of houses housed families from diverse cultures—Dutch, Puerto Rican, and many other Latino groups. Living among such rich human diversity was a great way to grow up, Ray says. He gained a respect for, and understanding of, all kinds of people. His parents taught him the importance of reading and writing at a young age, as a way to appreciate cultures throughout the world, and their customs, religions, and identities.

Even as Ray grew older and, eventually, got married and moved away from Brooklyn, he never lost the spirit of the place or forgot the unique experience of growing up in the *barrio*. In fact, he attributes his success to his parents and what he learned growing up in his old neighborhood.

Ray Suarez attended New York University, where he received a bachelor's degree in African history, and, later, a master's degree in social sciences from the University of Chicago, where he studied urban affairs.

Ray Suarez has subsequently been awarded honorary doctorates by Westminster College (Utah), and St. John's University (Minnesota).

"Never forget where you come from."

He landed his dream position, at *The NewsHour with Jim Lehrer* in October 1999, as a Washington-based senior correspondent. During his journey to this level, Ray says he witnessed the personal biases of some working in the media—especially, he contends, at prestigious news organizations. With his 25 years of varied experience, Ray noticed that the typical reporter profile was usually a young person who had the "right look for television." That meant there were few Latinos reporting the news. However, with his determination and insight, as well as his great ability to get along with others, Ray made his dream come true.

The way up to the top wasn't an easy one for Ray. He joined *Talk of the Nation* in 1993. Prior to that, he spent seven years covering local, national, and international stories for the NBC-owned station, WMAQ-TV, in Chicago. Even at that level, Ray remembers that only non-Latinos landed the more glamorous journalistic jobs. This didn't deter Ray; he simply rejected any stereotypes projected onto him. He went on to work as a Los Angeles correspondent for CNN, as a producer for the ABC Radio Network in New York, as a reporter for CBS Radio in Rome, and as a reporter for various American and British services in London.

Finally, though, his determination and perseverance won the day, when he became senior correspondent on *The NewsHour*. He attributes his success to his parents' support, and his father's hard work and the sacrifices he made to send his children to better schools. He feels that if other Latinos were similarly educated, in communities throughout the United States more and better job opportunities would open for Latinos.

21

Focus on What Is Right

JEFF GARCIA
Quarterback, National Football League

Successful people focus on one thing to excel at; this focus requires drive.

What does an athlete look like? Most people picture someone tall, athletically built, and muscle-bound. But this is not always the case, as Jeff Garcia proves.

Jeff is from Gilroy, California, a small town that promotes itself as the "garlic capital of the world." Driving through Gilroy with the windows rolled down, you can smell why this is so. This farming community is also proud of its most famous resident, professional football quarterback, Jeff Garcia.

Jeff is only half Mexican, yet he identifies primarily with that heritage, due to his father's influence. He believes it is the Hispanic culture and work ethic that sustained him as he began his ascent into professional football. It also helped him appreciate the dedication it takes to succeed, when given the opportunity. In addition to all his coaches, Jeff attributes his success to his parents, who laid a solid foundation for him early in his life. They set high standards and gave him confidence; in particular, his father never doubted Jeff could make it to the highest level in football.

Jeff's football career began in high school, where, he says, some of his classmates didn't think he was big enough to be an effective player. Jeff's response was to focus on what he *did* have: a powerful competitive spirit. He resolved to prove the skeptics wrong.

In college, Jeff became a quarterback on the San Jose State University team; there, he began to catch the attention of the fans, for he gave all he had in every game, and the result could be seen on the scoreboard. And his numbers on the record books kept mounting—for example, he received national recognition for his passing yardage during his last two years in college.

Jeff was a star off the field, too. He always believed it was just as important to dedicate himself to academic achievements as it was to accumulating athletic honors.

After college, Jeff's dream was to be drafted by one of the National Football League teams, but it didn't come true right away. Instead, he was selected to play for the Calgary Stampeders in the Canadian Football League. But after Jeff took that team to the 1998 Grey Cup Championship, ultimately winning it all, there was no stopping him. He had answered all questions about his size and lack of arm strength.

The following year, he again tried out for the NFL; this time he was picked up by the San Francisco 49ers. Though he failed to win a spot on the starting roster, another player's misfortune opened the door to Jeff's big chance. Early in the 1999 season, star quarterback Steve Young was sacked by Aeneas Williams and suffered a concussion, knocking him for the year. Jeff stepped in and finished the season. He played in thirteen games and made ten starts. The following season, with Young now retired, Jeff held onto the starting quarterback position and made his first Pro Bowl appearance. During the 2000 season, he set a new team record for passing yards, with 4,278. In each of the next two seasons, Jeff led the 49ers to the playoffs. Even more impressive, in the 2000 and 2001 seasons, he posted 31 and 30 passing touchdowns, respectively, more than any other 49er quarterback. This earned him the ranking as one of the top quarterbacks in the league. He went to the Pro Bowl in three consecutive seasons (2000–2002).

On March 15, 2006, Jeff signed a one-year contract with the Philadelphia Eagles to serve as the primary backup to Donovan McNabb. Once again, it was a season-ending injury to another player that put Jeff back in the limelight. Stepping in for McNabb as the starting quarterback, in eight games, he threw 10 touchdowns, and had only 2 interceptions, while posting a quarterback rating of 95.8. A year later, on January 7, 2007, Garcia earned his second playoff win, throwing for 153 yards and 1 touchdown in a 23–20 win over the New York Giants.

Jeff's new team is the Tampa Bay Buccaneers, an opportunity he is very excited about, because he has always wanted to play for Coach John Gruden.

"When faced with criticism, zone in on the solution."

Although today Jeff is playing for an East Coast team, his heart remains with the Hispanic community in the Bay Area. There, he is involved with the Hispanic Scholarship Fund (HSF), an organization that has raised a substantial amount of money to help deserving Hispanics pursue their college degrees. Jeff has been a member of the HSF for the past four years and a board member since 2005. Jeff says he feels rewarded every time he can give back to underrepresented neighborhoods—and he never forgets how blessed he is to have the resources to give back.

"To surround yourself with positive people, first find the leader within."

Another way he does that is to support other Latinos who have an interest in football as a career. This is important to Jeff, for though the ranks of Hispanic players are growing in the NFL, they still are not well represented, despite the NFL's documented efforts to achieve this objective. In that regard, Jeff tells young football players to focus equally on their academic careers as well as their athletic goals. Doing so, he says, will help them get admitted to good colleges, with coaches who can make a difference.

Jeff adds that it can be difficult to balance coursework with the demands of the game, so he stresses the importance for young players to surround themselves with positive, high-achieving people. And, he says, perseverance will win the day. He is living proof of that.

Jeff knows that his career in professional football has helped him to become a leader in the Hispanic community, where he is widely recognized as a role model of inspiration and hope to younger Latinos.

"Anyone can achieve the highest level of success; they only have to put in the effort."

22

Be in the Game

RONNIE LOPEZ

President of Phoenix International Consultants, and Chief of Staff for Former Arizona Governor, Bruce Babbitt

In order for the Latino voice to be heard, it is important for all Latinos to vote and be accounted for.

Ronnie Lopez's philosophy is that before Latinos can fully participate in their communities they first must know their rights and recognize that their voices, their votes, matter. Simply, to be heard, they must vote.

"Hard work goes a long way."

Ronnie's tenacious spirit and staunch belief in the power of the people has led to his successes in civil rights, politics, and business. He has served as a field representative of the Arizona Civil Rights Commission, and later worked as president and chief executive officer of Chicanos Por la Causa (for the cause). Ronnie also served as chief of staff and executive assistant to Governor Babbitt of Arizona, and as national deputy campaign manager for presidential candidate Walter Mondale.

Ronnie's strong sense of civic duty, coupled with his political savvy, has given him an edge in his pursuit of a multifaceted career as an entrepreneur and political consultant. Today, Ronnie is the president of Phoenix International Consultants, a lobbying and public relations firm, with clients such as Southwest Airlines, Cigna Healthcare, the Phoenix Coyotes, and the William Mercer Company. He also sits on the board of directors for the Congressional Hispanic Caucus Institute, and serves as the finance chairman for Congressman Ed Pastor. He is also the director for Bank of America in Arizona.

In spite of all his success, Ronnie continues to believe society's true heroes and role models are the too-often-overlooked gardeners, hotel room cleaning men and women, busboys and waitstaff, and other under-appreciated laborers. This view stems from his own humble beginnings, and his subsequent work with the people he represents, who, he says, sacrifice daily to provide a better life for their children and future generations.

23

Flex Your Intellectual Muscle

MARTIN CABRERA
President and CEO, Cabrera Capital Markets

Life lessons are most often learned through early experiences.

Martin Cabrera grew up in Chicago, Illinois, and as a young child often worked selling used goods in flea markets. He remembers how the items he sold would put a smile on the faces of his customers. Keeping busy and working hard, he says, kept him from falling prey to a life on the streets of his tough neighborhood, where gangs and drugs prevailed.

"Stay busy and focused."

Though humble, Martin's work in the flea market proved to be valuable experience, for it was there he learned to negotiate and understand the concept of selling and bidding; he also learned the importance of making the customer happy.

But it was a game he played in high school that changed his life forever. In an economics class, they played the Stock Market Exchange Game (SMEG), which is sponsored by the Securities Industry Association. SMEG was more than just a classroom game, however; it was a competition among schools throughout the city of Chicago. The winning team was the one that earned the highest return on investment.

It was this game, coupled with a passion for numbers, that inspired Martin to pursue a degree in finance, from Northern Illinois University. At the young age of 30, through tenacity and perseverance, he bought his first brokerage firm in Wisconsin, which was reincorporated in Illinois. Today, Cabrera Capital Markets is a successful full-service brokerage firm that manages U.S. and international equities portfolios for its clients. With offices in nine different cities, Cabrera Capital is now one of the top Illinois-based brokerage firms. Financial transactions happen at a hectic pace in this competitive market. Cabrera Capital Markets executes transactions directly on the floor at all the major stock market exchanges through a state-of-the-art electronic trading system, which enables staff to route trades in the marketplace in a manner that is most advantageous to the clients.

Martin, however, takes as much pride in the effort he makes to give back to the Latino community, primarily in the form of scholarships. In addition, Cabrera Capital Markets contributed $50,000 to expand the Stock Market Game Program in the Chicago public school system so that other young children learn they, too, can be successful in the rough-and-tumble, competitive financial marketplace. For this focus, he credits his father and role model. He has childhood memories of his father's generosity: He would donate clothes to other families, provide bus tickets to those who could not afford them, take in people who did not have a place to stay. Martin never forgot these many acts of kindness.

24

Achievements That Keep Growing

MIRIAM RIVERA
Former Vice President and Deputy General Counsel, Google, Inc.

Never give up on your dreams, even when obstacles present themselves.

B y the time Miriam Rivera was in her early forties, she had a lifetime of achievements to her credit, and had earned the respect and admiration of her attorney colleagues across the United States. Her experience as vice president and deputy general counsel at Google, Inc. gave her the chance to assist with two follow-on offerings there, which raised approximately $6 billion; the first, in 2005, at $4 billion, was the largest ever follow-on in the United States; the second, in 2006, occurred upon Google's admission to the S&P 500. At Google, Rivera was also responsible for some of the largest commercial deals completed in Silicon Valley to date. These included a deal in excess of $5 billion, as well as several at over $1 billion each. Miriam also provided legal support, in the form of contracting models, deal structures, and documentation for all of Google's revenue. During Miriam's tenure with the search engine giant, she saw the company grow from 160 to 10,000 employees, in addition to thousands of contractors; and saw annual revenue grow from $80 million to an estimated $10 billion.

Hard to believe this powerhouse attorney grew up in very humble circumstances on the rough north side of Chicago, where she was raised by her mother, an immigrant from Puerto Rico who worked in factories to provide for Miriam and her siblings. Her mother was a role model for the importance of a good education, for despite being a single mom with five children, and working full-time, she completed her eighth-grade diploma. And several years later, while in her fifties, she went on to earn her General Education Diploma (GED).

"A mother's unconditional support is all the inspiration a person needs to succeed."

Her mother's example fueled Miriam's determination to do well in school. At eleven, she was identified as a gifted student, and later was admitted to Phillips Exeter Academy, a prestigious boarding school in Exeter, New Hampshire. Miriam says she felt out of place initially in her new surroundings, especially upon walking into the Park Hyatt Hotel for her admissions interview. She recalls thinking, "Wow, I didn't know anyone but a guest could enter a hotel." Once inside, she noticed the people in business attire in the hotel lobby, imagining they must all have good educations that enabled them to get jobs that brought them to the hotel for business.

Eventually, however, Miriam returned to Chicago to finish high school, at the Latin School of Chicago. While still a student, Miriam held down a job at her neighborhood McDonald's, sometimes working until midnight or later. The long hours were one thing, but more difficult to tolerate was having to wait on the rich kids from her high school, who went through the drive-through in their own cars. Little did they know that it was a future successful attorney who was serving them burgers.

Miriam went on to earn four degrees: a doctor of jurisprudence from Stanford Law School, a master of business administration from the Stanford Graduate School of Business, and a bachelor's degree in sociology and a master's degree in Spanish from Stanford University.

Miriam's success has been widely recognized. She has been the recipient of various prestigious awards, among them the Corporate Executive of the Year for Hispanic Net, Latina Attorney of the Year for the Hispanic National Bar Association, Woman of the Year (finalist) for *Hispanic Business* magazine, and a Top 10 In-house Lawyer Most Likely to Become General Counsel at a Fortune 500 Company in the Next Five Years from *Corporate Counsel* magazine.

Today, Miriam advises several start-up companies and nonprofit organizations, and serves on the Board of Visitors of Stanford Law School. She also has been nominated to the Stanford University Board of Trustees.

25

People Are Always Watching You

MARIA CONTRERAS-SWEET
Chairwoman and CEO, Promerica Bank

When you least expect it, people will be watching your performance.

Today, Latinos and other minorities nationwide are taking the plunge into the exciting world of entrepreneurship. Maria Contreras-Sweet is one such entrepreneur. In 2006, she opened Promerica Bank, the first new Latino-owned bank in Los Angeles, California, in more than 35 years. The mission of Promerica Bank is to give Latinos a place to take care of all their banking needs, in an atmosphere of acceptance and understanding of their culture.

Born in Guadalajara, Mexico, Maria's parents separated when she was five, leaving her mother to care for Maria and her four siblings. Her mother brought her young family to Los Angeles, California, where Maria grew up—though she says retains fond memories of Mexico and her pride in her roots. Some of her most treasured moments are those spent with her *abuelita* (grandmother), who taught Maria the importance of reading, and always took time to read the classics to her. It was her *abuelita* who also gave her advice she has never forgotten: "People are always watching you."

Maria went on to obtain a degree in political science from California State University, Los Angeles, after which she began her career in the political arena. This eventually led to her appointment by former Governor Gray Davis as his cabinet secretary for the California Business

Transportation and Housing (BT&H) Agency. She was the first Latina in the history of the state of California to hold this position.

As head of the BT&H Agency, Maria managed more than 40,000 employees and a budget of $14 billion. The agency was responsible for reconstructing the San Francisco–Oakland Bay Bridge, increasing the availability of affordable housing, and creating new jobs. She and her staff also launched the first Managed Healthcare Department in California. Maria then chaired the 2000 Census, giving her, she says, an amazing opportunity to take into account the people often overlooked: minorities. As a result of her work on the census, the state received new funding and gained another congressional seat.

"Latinos must feel that they are investing their money in a safe place."

It was this wide-ranging professional background and the contacts she made over the years that enabled Maria to secure the financial backing she needed to start Promerica Bank. Early to come onboard with the enterprise was Henry Cisneros, former U.S. Secretary of Housing; Solomon Trujillo, CEO of Telstra Communications; and music entrepreneur Rodi Rodriguez. Her idea continued to gain momentum and support until, in November 2006, Promerica Bank—the promise of America—opened its doors.

Promerica Bank was a much-needed resource in the Latino community. Before it opened, Latino and other minority entrepreneurs had few, if any, sources for sound business and financial advice. Promerica staff teach them how to use the capital in their businesses and help them to acquire new loans to keep their businesses viable until they become profitable.

Maria's heart has always been with the Latino community. In addition to her business ventures, she also has founded Hispanics Organized for Political Equality (HOPE), which today has attracted prominent Latinas, lawmakers, and others who whose common goal is to help integrate the Latin American view into mainstream society, especially in schools.

IV

Unique Ability

It is all too easy to stay in your comfort zone and do what you have always done, in the same way you have always done it, especially when faced with challenging or demanding situations, whether in business, sports, or relationships. But being successful requires taking risks and pushing yourself, sometimes to the limit.

In this effort, the first step is to assess your goals, and on your path to achieving them, start with what you are naturally good at. That is, know yourself; play to your strengths, and understand how they can help you make your dreams come true. Resist the temptation to blend in to the crowd; rather, be willing to stand out. Learn to be comfortable in your own skin. It is only once you understand yourself and what you are capable of that you will be able to leverage your power to achieve success.

Most important, be willing to share your unique abilities with others.

26

The Vision Is Alive

CHEECH MARIN
Actor, Comic, Artist

Giving back to the community is an enriching and rewarding experience.

Richard Anthony Marin was born in South Central Los Angeles, California. As a child, one of his uncles said he looked like a *chicharron*, a piece of spicy fried pigskin. The comparison became a nickname, shortened to "Cheech." He has been known as that ever since.

Like so many in the Latino community, Cheech was challenged from the beginning simply by virtue of growing up in a tough neighborhood. And like so many others, his early experiences gave him the drive to succeed. Cheech was fortunate, too, to have solid support from his parents. His father encouraged Cheech to go to college; in fact, he told him he was *expected* to pursue his education. So in the 1960s, Cheech headed to college.

He began his showbiz career as a stand-up comic, in the late 1960s in Los Angeles, where he was discovered in a nightclub performing with his soon-to-be movie partner, Tommy Chong.

"Never give up on your dreams."

By the eighties, he had transitioned into moviemaking. In 1987, Cheech wrote, directed, and starred in the comedy, *Born in East L.A.*, with Paul Rodriguez. At that time, it was rare to see Latinos, specifically Mexican-Americans, as leading film characters. He subsequently appeared in supporting roles in *Tin Cup*, with Kevin Costner, as well as *Spy Kids* and *Christmas with the Kranks*. Cheech also costarred in *Once Upon a Time in Mexico*, with Johnny Depp, Antonio Banderas, and Salma Hayek; and in *Spy Kids 3*, with Antonio Banderas. He starred in Robert Rodriguez's film, *From Dusk Till Dawn;* and in *Desperado*, again with Antonio Banderas. He has also lent his voice to animated films, as one of the hyenas in Disney's *The Lion King*, and as one of the autos in the Pixar film, *Cars*.

Cheech later became a familiar face on television. He played a police officer on the television series *Nash Bridges*, with Don Johnson, and had a recurring role on the series *Judging Amy*.

But Cheech is much more than a Hollywood celebrity. In his spare time, he volunteers for the Hispanic Scholarship Fund, and serves on the Inner City Arts Council. He is a collector of Latino art, and helped create the Chicano art represented in "Chicano Vision." Cheech, who considers himself a Chicano, has a mission: to share with all Americans, of all cultures, what Chicano art means to this country.

"Give back to the Latino community."

Cheech is an artist, too. His own art was recently on display at the M. H. deYoung museum in San Francisco, California, then traveled, between 2006 and 2007, to fifteen other museums throughout the country, as well as two abroad. It may truly be said that Cheech Marin is a Renaissance man.

27

Believe in Your Dreams

SUSIE CASTILLO
Former Miss USA, Actress

In life, it is important to have the drive for success and the passion for internal happiness.

In 2003, Susie Castillo became the third Latina to be crowned Miss USA. As smart as she is beautiful, and a true role model to Latinas across the country, she went on to college and became the second person in her family to earn a degree, a bachelor's in interior architecture and design from Endicott College, where her senior thesis won her a Capstone Award, given to one graduating senior.

In the Spanish-speaking neighborhood where she spent her childhood, Susie says her only role model was her mother, a single parent who worked hard in and outside the home, and taught her daughter that no goal or dream was out of reach. Susie took that philosophy to heart, which made all the difference between her future and that of other Latina girls in her neighborhood. Susie watched many of them give into peer pressure or get caught up in the cycle of early teenage pregnancy, making their chances of succeeding very slim.

"Reach your full potential."

After being crowned Miss USA 2003, Susie sought a career in acting She has appeared in various sitcoms, such as *My Wife and Kids*, and in 2007, she starred in the movie, *The Underdog*. Currently, she is a co-host on MTV.

In her spare time, Susie champions the cause of education for young Latina woman. She is passionate in this effort, and is committed to continuing to serve as a role model for other young women who need support as they struggle to achieve their own goals.

28

Believe in a Great Script

MOCTESUMA ESPARZA
Executive Producer and CEO, Maya Films

Having a voice in the Latino community is a strong tool for success.

Moctesuma Esparza has always been something of a visionary in the Latino community. As a student at the University of California, Los Angeles, in the late 1960s, he was outspoken at a time when many Latinos and Chicanos were reluctant to step up to the challenge, for fear of rocking the boat. He was determined to voice his opinions despite what the general public thought. Moctesuma played an active role in forming Movimiento Estudiantil Chicano de Aztlan, MECHA, an organization whose mission was to implement a plan of action to build an educational ladder for the advancement of Chicanos. He also was a leader during the Chicano Student Walkouts of 1968.

Even as he was participating actively on campus, he excelled in his studies, eventually receiving his bachelor's and master's degrees in theater arts—motion pictures and television—from UCLA.

His political activism grew in conjunction with his film career. Moctesuma was on-site with a film crew at the August 1970 National Moratorium March against the Vietnam War. The footage he shot there was incorporated into the film *Requiem 29*.

Decades later, in 2006, he produced the movie *The Walkout*, directed by Edward James Olmos. Other notable productions are *The Ballad of Gregorio Cortez* and *The Milagro Beanfield War*. But perhaps his best-known film is the 1997 hit, *Selena*, starring Jennifer Lopez.

"Don't be afraid of challenges."

Moctesuma has been one of the pioneer Latinos in the film industry for more than thirty years now, with the kudos to prove it. He has received more than 200 awards and recognitions for his work, including an Emmy for *Cinco Vidas* (Best Film, Best Writer), an Academy Award nomination for *Agueda Martinez—Our People, Our Country*, a Clio Award for the public service announcement "Drunk Drivers Get Carried Away," and a Golden Globe and Emmy nomination for *Introducing Dorothy Dandridge* (Best Television Movie).

Also an entrepreneur, Moctesuma acquired a franchise in the first Latino-owned cable company, Buenavision Cable TV, in East Los Angeles, and he owns a chain of movie theater complexes, called Maya Cinemas.

Moctesuma also has served as chair of the board of the New America Alliance, and is president, CEO, executive vice president, and major stockholder of Maya Cinemas North American, Inc., Saints & Sinners Film Development Co., Inc., Esparza/Katz Productions, Inc., Moctesuma Esparza Productions, Inc., Buenavision Telecommunications, Inc., and Buenavision Telecommunications of Boyle Heights, Inc.

"Be part of the big picture."

Moctesuma has never let his professional career interfere with his involvement in the Latino community. His impact in the public service sector is notable. He has served as chair on several boards of directors, including the Cesar Chavez Foundation Corporate Board of Directors and the National Hispanic Media Coalition Board of Directors. He was a founding member of the National Association of Latino Producers and the Los Angeles Academy of Arts and Enterprise Charter School. He has been recognized for his service to the community, receiving the Cesar Chavez Award from the Association of Mexican American Educators, the Champion of Hope Award from Hispanics Organized for Political Equality, the Los Angeles City Council's Commendation for Public Service, and the Congressional Hispanic Institute's Medallion of Excellence.

29

Be Prepared for the Bell to Ring

LOU MORET
Professional Boxing Referee; Professor, Pepperdine University

Education provides hope to those who are at an economic disadvantage.

L ou Moret has a unique perspective on what it means to be successful: he believes that wherever you are—in school, at work, or in the boxing ring—the key to success is to always be prepared for the bell to ring. That is, be ready to roll with the punches, recognize that life requires you to adjust your attitude on a regular basis, based on what is going on around you. If you are not prepared in this way, and learn to move swiftly, life's challenges will surely defeat you.

Lou grew up in a low-income neighborhood of East Los Angeles, California. The odds seemed stacked against him. He compares life there to living on an island of negative influences, with little emphasis on education. Still, he completed high school, and came away with the knowledge that he would need to become disciplined if he was to succeed in life.

"It's never too late to aim for the top."

For that discipline, Lou turned to the U.S. Army. His experiences in the armed forces fueled his desire to continue his education, which he did, at East Los Angeles Community College, eventually receiving his bachelor of arts in sociology from Whittier College, his master of policy analysis from the University of Southern California, and a doctorate of policy analysis from the University of La Verne.

That education laid the foundation for great things to come, notably Lou's nomination in 1979 by President Jimmy Carter, and confirmation by the United States Senate, to serve as the first director of the Office of Minority Economic Impact in the Department of Energy. There, he advised the secretary of energy on matters of the economic and environmental impact of the department's policy on the poor and disadvantaged in the United States. Needless to say, growing up with very few resources himself gave Lou a personal understanding for those at an economic disadvantage.

Lou now has more than 30 years experience in politics and administration, specializing in private sector management, to his credit. He has served as the commissioner of the Los Angeles Department of Public Works, chief of staff for Assemblyman Richard Alatorre, and deputy director for the United States of Minority Business Enterprise. In 1999, he retired as chief operating officer of the Southern California Association of Governments, the largest regional planning organization in the United States. He was also a member of the Democratic National Committee, from 1981 to 1993, served as chair of the Hispanic Caucus from 1982 to 1984, and sat on the board of directors of the Congressional Hispanic Caucus Institute, from 1985 to 1990.

Lou's deep interest in with the Latino community continues, and he now empowers this fastest-growing minority in the United States by working as a visiting lecturer on business courses at Pepperdine University.

But government and community development are not Lou's only passion. He also loves boxing, and has become a professional referee. In that capacity, he has officiated at fights featuring boxing greats Oscar De La Hoya, Evander Holyfield, and Lennox Lewis, as well as countless other world champions. He even "starred" as one of the boxing officials in Clint Eastwood's Academy Award-winning movie *Million Dollar Baby*.

30

From Santee to Stanford

MARGARITA QUIHUIS
President and CEO, Hispanic–Net

Family support is one of the most important elements of success.

W hen Margarita Quihuis left Santee, California, to begin her college career, she did not go alone. Her proud parents drove her to Palo Alto, home to Stanford University, where Margarita would earn her bachelor of science in petroleum engineering. But that day, as they walked her to her apartment, with all her belongings, it was all they could do not to cry. It was only after giving her a hug and heading back home that her mother gave way to tears.

Stanford would mark a great change in Margarita's life, in more ways than one. In Santee, where had spent her childhood, the population is composed primarily of diverse lower-income ethnic groups, with a large influence of Yaquis Indians and Mexicans. Margarita's heritage is both—her mother is a Mexican from Zacatecas, and her father is a Yaquis Indian. In Palo Alto, the demographics are notably different, predominantly made up of the affluent white, upper-middle class. It was a world of difference to Margarita, who had long been an observer of cultures and people.

"Observing cultures brings a sense of self and pride."

Margarita considers herself a social entrepreneur. Today, she is the president and CEO of Hispanic–Net, the culmination of a very wide-ranging career. She has been involved in developing high-end aerospace systems and gender-focused design; she was also founder of Indigo Financiera. Her credentials also include venture capitalist and Reuters Fellow at Stanford University, where she became a subject matter expert on remittances for development.

Highlights of her experience include financial innovation for those unserved or underserved by the banking community, both in the United States and in developing countries. She is also instrumental in encouraging technological innovation on behalf of humanitarian needs. She was named as one of the Women in Technology International (WITI) Women to Watch in 2003; in 2004, thanks to her efforts to offer women entrepreneurs greater access to capital, Margarita was recognized by *Women's eNews* magazine as one of their 21 Leaders for the 21st Century.

Margarita maintains a venture advisory practice, where she uses her private equity experience and network to transition prefunded and early-stage start-up companies into viable, fundable, and sustainable businesses. She has a special interest in firms whose overall market or objective is sustainability, triple bottom line, or a base of the pyramid (BoP) focus (dealing with the world's 4 billion poor). Previously, Margarita was a venture partner for NewVista Capital, a seed and early-stage venture fund focused on the information technology and enterprise software markets. Margarita led the due diligence efforts for new investments in the enterprise software, Internet infrastructure, wireless, and educational software markets, and sat on or observed the boards of several New Vista portfolio companies, including Epicentric, Reach Communications, Bridgestream, Broadware, and ZNYX.

From 1999 to 2001, Margarita was the founding executive director of the San Francisco-based Women's Technology Cluster (WTC). Recognized as one of the top business incubators in the country by Red Herring and eCompany, the WTC specializes in helping launch high-tech, life science, and social enterprise companies that are run by women. The WTC became a key go-to laboratory for international delegations, and was used as an example for incubation efforts in Malaysia, Scandinavia, Eastern Europe, and Latin America. Through her highly visible work with this organization, Margarita has emerged as both a national advocate for women's entrepreneurship in high technology and an expert on new models for high-tech economic development, entrepreneurship, and venture funding. During her tenure, WTC portfolio companies raised $67 million in private equity. Margarita has served as a consultant to the U.S. State Department on entrepreneurship, and has been widely quoted in the *Asian Venture Capital Report*, *The NewsHour with Jim Lehrer*, *US News & World Report*, *Forbes ASAP*, *Red Herring*, *CNN*, and *CBS MarketWatch*. She is the founder of 1st Wednesdays, the network for women in venture capital. From 1995 to 2000, she served as a board member of the Forum for Women Entrepreneurs, and was a member of the screening and coaching committees for Springboard 2000, the venture capital conference for women. Margarita is a past board member of NanoSig, a northern California-based organization dedicated to the commercialization of nanotechnology.

She currently sits on the boards of Agent Software, Women's eNews, Hispanic–Net, and the James Burke Institute, and is on the advisory boards of Acrossworld Communications and Merrill Lynch's Latino Advisory Council. She was also part of the founding working group for the Business Women's Initiative on AIDS.

Clearly, Margarita Quihuis took her father's advice to "be excellent" to heart.

31

Dream Big

HECTOR BARRETO JR.
Former Administrator, U.S. Small Business Administration

No one can succeed alone.

Hector Barreto's father came to the United States in the 1950s. His first job was digging potatoes on a farm near Corning, Missouri, for 80 cents an hour. But he managed to save his pennies and open his first restaurant, Mexico Lindo, which over time became a successful multimillion dollar chain. Barreto, Sr. also founded, and served as president of, the United States Hispanic Chamber of Commerce. He was later named chairman emeritus of the organization. He is a member of the League of Latin American Citizens' (LULAC) Hall of Fame. The U.S. Hispanic Chamber of Commerce has established a scholarship in his honor.

With a role model like that, it's no wonder his son has become such a success.

"Every penny counts."

As a young man, Hector helped his parents manage their businesses—the restaurant, an export/import business, and a construction company in Kansas City, Missouri, his hometown. Those experiences, and the success of his father, prepared him well for future leadership. His father's legacy inspired Hector to follow his dreams, which he shares today not only with the Latino leaders in America but all Americans.

"The legacy of a great parent will drive you to succeed."

Barreto, Jr. also shares his father's entrepreneurial and community spirit. He, too, became a business owner, and served as vice chairman of the board for the U.S. Hispanic Chamber of Commerce. He gained managerial experience by working for the Miller Brewing Company, as the South Texas area manager. In California, he founded an employees' benefit firm, which specialized in financial services for southern California's rapidly growing population. He served as chairman of the board for the Latino Business Association in Los Angeles, and *Hispanic Business Magazine* named him one of America's 100 Most Influential Hispanics.

In July 2001, President George W. Bush nominated Hector Barreto, Jr. as the twenty-first administrator of the Small Business Administration (SBA). The SBA is responsible for managing a portfolio of direct and guaranteed business and disaster loans worth more than $45 billion, which makes it the largest facilitator in areas of technical assistance for the nation's small businesses. The Senate unanimously confirmed the nomination, making Hector the highest-ranking small business advocate in the country. In this capacity, he oversaw the delivery of financial and business development tools to America's entrepreneurs.

"Make the Hispanic community proud by working hard."

Hector is happy to see the number of Latino leaders in this country growing, especially among elected officials and teachers. Likewise, he points to the importance of mentoring programs like the New America Alliance, which are coming together to create business opportunities for Latinos in the United States. As Hector knows, no one can succeed alone—all individuals need the support of their community, as well as personal or professional networks. Following in his father's footsteps as a role model, he tells young people to set high standards for themselves and their communities, and it becomes a win-win situation: The community helps individuals succeed, and individuals help the community succeed.

32

The Language of Culture

ISABEL VALDES
Entrepreneur, Author, Consultant, and Public Speaker

It's not a matter of language; it's a matter of culture.

Isabel Valdez was fortunate to be exposed to academia at a young age. She was taught as a child that the only way to succeed in life was by getting an education. By age four, Isabel had already learned what it's like to live in a very different culture than her own, for her family had to move from Chile to Germany where her father went to work on his advanced degree in biochemistry. By the time Isabel was ready for her own graduate education, she traveled to yet a third cultural environment, the United States, where she came as both a Fulbright and Ford Foundation scholar. At Stanford University, she earned two master of arts degrees, in communications and education. She also holds professional degrees in communications and communications arts and advertising from two leading universities in South America.

For almost a decade, Isabel conducted communications research for Stanford University, and was a member of the clinical faculty at Stanford University School of Medicine's Division of Family Medicine, where she gained first-hand knowledge of the grass-roots Latino community in rural and urban areas.

"Start at a grass-roots level and work your way up."

Ultimately, though, Isabel chose to turn her experiences gained while living in vastly different cultures into the highly valuable assets that led to her successful career today as one of the few Latinas in the world who specializes in Hispanic and cross cultural marketing. In fact, she has developed a niche in this field she is passionate about.

For the last 25 years, Isabel's business motto has been: "It's not just a matter of language, but culture." As she explains: "Every consumer, across countries, market segments, or communities, wants the same things from life: a stable income, a nice home and car, a family that has access to a middle-class lifestyle, good health care, inner joy, peace, and social respect. However, the way members of different cultures—within the United States and around the globe—experience and enjoy life, express their needs, wants, dreams, and fears, is unique to each culture." Isabel believes that the more business and marketing managers learn about cultural differences—and then how to capitalize on them, with respect—the greater their chances for success in this marketplace.

A seasoned entrepreneur, Isabel founded, and managed for 15 years, a marketing research company, Hispanic Market Connections, Inc., where she devised state-of-the-art marketing research methods that became standard in the industry. These include the National Hispanic Database, the first national study of its kind to incorporate cultural and psychosocial variables to develop an in-culture psychographic platform to market and manage product and service portfolios with acculturating Latino consumer segments. She is recognized as the founder of the in-culture marketing approach.

Later, as president of the Cultural Access Group, she directed the national management reorganization for Chase Manhattan Bank to better serve its growing nationwide Hispanic business. She helped take the company public, in 1998.

"It's not just a matter of language, but culture."

Isabel has established herself as a pioneer in cross cultural marketing and consulting; she is also an author, popular public speaker, and consultant. She has consulted with corporations throughout the United States and abroad for the past three decades.

Isabel has also created many of today's standard best practices and tools in multicultural and inner-city research, such as HMC's Language Segmentation model, the first generational-based segmentation model, the first zip-code-based financial value segmentation analysis, the Culture Market Opportunity Assessment, visual icon probing technology, and many others.

In addition, she developed the basic business model and research design for A.C. Nielson's Hispanic Household Panel, the largest longitudinal, ongoing multicultural panel in the United States. It is utilized by blue-chip corporations. Her client list includes nonprofit government organizations and a long list of service, entertainment, media, and consumer product companies, among them Procter & Gamble, Universal Studios, AT&T, regional public utilities, telephone and cellular companies, Coca-Cola, General Mills, Kraft, Bank of America, Time Warner, Univision and Telemundo, La Opinion, VISA International, Allstate, State Farm, Honda of America, and many others.

Currently, she is a member of PepsiCo/Frito-Lay's Latino Advisory Board, and the Advisory Board of Scholastic, Lee y Serás. She is also a member of the Advisory Board for Consumer Trends Forum International. In addition, Isabel is an active member in the Hispanic community, as a board member for the National Council of La Raza and the Latino Community Foundation, San Francisco.

Isabel has received numerous honors, including selection by Fortune Small Business, in 2001, as a Woman Entrepreneur Star, and Business Woman of the Year by the New York Hispanic Chambers of Commerce in 1995. In March 2000, she was named by *American Demographics* magazine as the 21st Century Star of Multicultural Research, and three years later was given the Visionary Award 2003 by the San Francisco Hispanic Chamber of Commerce and the University of San Francisco.

As an expert in her field, Isabel has written a number of books, the two most recent of which extend the in-culture methodology to the general market and other multicultural market segments. One, released in 2002, is titled *Marketing to American Latinos, A Guide to the In-Culture Approach, Part 2* (Paramount Market Publishing). The most recent is *Hispanic Consumers for Life: A Fresh Look of Acculturation* (Paramount Market Publishing, 2008).

33

Surround Yourself with Positive People

RUDY BESERRA
Vice President of Latin Affairs, Coca-Cola

Establish friendships and strong networks in your personal and professional life.

Rudy Bessera attributes his success to his grandfather, whose philosophy was that success begins when you respect your community and learn to be proud of who you are. When you do that, Rudy's grandfather believed, a person will gain pride and dignity, and inevitably be surrounded by successful people. The formula of success, his grandfather told him, was to start by choosing the right friends and then build a network of peers in your field for support and to share knowledge.

"Create a positive network."

Rudy is a second-generation Mexican-American who grew up in Albuquerque, New Mexico. His grandparents emigrated from the states of Chihuahua and Zacatecas, Mexico. Living in a lower-income neighborhood as a young child taught Rudy to appreciate those who were willing to work hard in life, and didn't take things for granted.

After graduating high school, Rudy was accepted to the University of New Mexico in Albuquerque, where he received a bachelor's degree, with a minor in political science, along with his teaching credentials. He began working as a counselor, then transitioned into sales. His experience in business sales opened the door to the political arena, where Rudy became the small business and Hispanic liaison to the Republican National Committee.

Rudy began his political career as the Associate Director of Public Liaison to the Hispanic, Asian, and Arab-American communities. On August 25, 1988, President Ronald Reagan appointed Rudy as Special Assistant to the President as Public Liaison. Throughout his years working with the Republican party, Rudy learned valuable leadership skills, based on principles that he believes in to this day: creating employment opportunities, maintaining respect for family values, and fostering a sense of community involvement and parental empowerment.

After leaving political life, in 1989, Rudy began his career at the Coca-Cola Company. The first thing visitors notice when they walk into his office is a black-and-white photograph of his grandfather and father, taken in the 1930s in a grocery store. Behind the displays of bananas and soda bottles is a sign advertising Coca-Cola. Every morning, Rudy looks at the photo and thinks, "Life is good," and sometimes wonders if he was destined to work for the soft-drink giant.

"Always pay attention to the signs of a great opportunity."

Rudy attributes his success at Coca-Cola to the skills he learned through his involvement in such organizations and boards as the League of United Latin American Citizens (LULAC), the Office of Civil Rights–New Mexico, and the Republican National Committee.

V

Resiliency

In life, it is inevitable that people will encounter setbacks. It is those individuals with tenacious spirits who bounce back after facing adversity and go on to achieve their goals. In this way, successful people become resilient, and, more, learn to take advantage of setbacks and turn them into opportunities for growth. Setbacks offer valuable time and space for introspection, to reexamine one's goals and reevaluate how to achieve them.

Tenacity and resiliency are closely linked characteristics, giving determined individuals the strength they need to stay on track toward achieving their objectives, yet be flexible enough to navigate the rough waters that will come their way. Successful people also know when to ask for feedback, and for help and support when they need it.

34

Living a Farmworker's Dream

MARTIN R. CURIEL
Vice President, Marketing, Denali Advisors, LLC

Hard work teaches people the importance of teamwork.

Martin Curiel was born in Yuba, California. His family were farm-workers, who labored six months of the year in the fields of the Sacramento Valley, alternately picking peaches, plums, cherries, almonds, and olives. His fondest memories of growing up in this agricultural region were of working side by side with his siblings and parents, even though they never had a stable home, living as they did in farm-camps.

At a young age, Martin learned the meaning of resiliency from his father, Francisco Curiel, who, Martin remembers, was always the first worker in the field in the morning and the last to break for lunch. Martin also learned the value of teamwork and networking from his father, who often organized work efforts on behalf of the other laborers. Martin's father had the extraordinary ability to direct people, at the same time he made them feel good about a hard day's work, and take pleasure in a job well done.

From his father's example, Martin developed a strong work ethic. He learned that, to see results, one simply has to work hard, and be willing to take responsibility for one's own future. He saw too, the value of dedication in reaching for his dream.

In the early 1990s, Martin was accepted at the California Polytechnic University in San Luis Obispo, California. Of course, his father was there to drive him to college. Together, with seven other passengers, Martin climbed into his father's truck for the trip from Oregon. But fate interceded that day, to test Martin's resolve and faith. A semidiesel crossed into the lane they were driving in and hit their truck. The impact was so powerful that five of the passengers died at the scene, including Martin's father. Two others were sent to intensive care. Martin, however, was spared; he walked away with just scratches—and an everlasting vision of the horrific accident. But Martin became resilient that day, as he whispered to himself, "Father, I will never let you down, I will succeed in college."

And so he did. He earned his bachelor's degree in engineering, and scored well on the GMAT exam. Then, after gaining a few years' experience in business, Martin decided to aim for the top: He applied to Harvard School of Business. In 2002, he was accepted to that prestigious institution, and went on to earn his MBA from there.

"Leadership is the ability to lead others to do that which others choose not to do."

Today, Martin is the founder of the Rising Farmworker Dream Fund, a nonprofit organization whose mission is to empower U.S. farmworkers, and improve their social and financial positions. To that end, the organization provides business sector resources to enable positive change within this underserved population. Martin would also like to see an increase in access to human, social, and financial capital within communities throughout the United States.

"On the ladder to success, keep one hand up, reaching for the top, and the other reaching down, to help those behind you."

Francisco Curiel continues to inspire his son, and through his son, others. In 1993, Martin established a memorial fund in honor of his father, to benefit other farmworkers' children who have lost their parents.

35

Keep a Sense of Pride

MARILOU MARTINEZ STEVENS
President and CEO, MMS

Dressing for success helps position you for that dream job.

Marilou Martinez Stevens remembers moving to the United States with her family when she was about nine. Her parents had decided to leave Mexico in order to give their children a better chance to succeed. Although her parents both had professional occupations in Mexico—her father was a pharmacist and her mother a teacher—they had to start from scratch when they arrived in this country. Their first home here was in a predominantly Spanish-speaking, low-income neighborhood in Poteet, Texas, where they shared an apartment with her aunt. The building they lived in was run by slumlords, and the residents had to endure daily the moldy, rancid stench of decay and neglect as they walked down the hallways.

Marilou remembers crowding into this tightly shared space with her two sisters and parents as if it were yesterday. All the family's possessions had to be crammed into one small bedroom. So small were the living quarters that she and her sisters had to take turns sitting down for meals at the kitchen table. The standard bill of fare was the typical Latino diet: beans, rice, and, occasionally, cheese (a block of processed yellow cheese provided free by the U.S. government).

Even in these dire circumstances, however, Marilou said her father maintained his pride, which was always apparent from his appearance—he always dressed up. Even at home, he looked dapper—he may have been poor, but he never looked poor. In this way, he demonstrated to his daughters that these living conditions were only temporary.

Marilou also recalls her father's determination to master the English language and do well in business, so that he could become a valuable participant in this new culture. His first job was as an insurance salesman, which required him to go door to door. With his rich spirit and fierce passion, he soon excelled, so much so that he was given an American National award in recognition of his achievements. With her father as a positive role model, Marilou's life began to change, and she began to believe that she could do anything in life.

"Emotional support goes a long way."

When Marilou began to talk about going to college, her parents provided the emotional support that gave her the courage to ask a high school counselor how to proceed in this effort. Moreover, she had proven herself to be a hard worker, and had the good grades to show for it. Nevertheless, the counselor wasn't encouraging about her prospects for attending college, and Marilou went home disappointed and in despair. But her mother turned her right around again, saying, *"Si mija quiere ir, va ir al colegio"* ("If my daughter wants to go to college, she will go to college").

Sure enough, she did. And with perseverance, her parents' encouragement, and hard work, she graduated from the University of Texas at Austin with degrees in accounting and computer programming. Then, in true entrepreneurial spirit, at the tender age of 26, and with only a few years of experience, Marilou founded her first company, Medical Data Management (MDM), an accounting firm focused on assisting medical practitioners with financial reporting and various accounting procedures. In 1987, she sold MDM and joined the accounting department at General Dynamic Corporation as a senior financial analyst. She also continued to educate herself, receiving her certification of public accountancy (CPA) and a 7 Broker and Group Insurance license.

In 1991, Marilou moved to Virginia, where she founded her own accounting firm, Marilou Martinez Stevens (MMS), a certified public accounting firm engaged in providing accounting, tax, and consulting services, as well as special-purpose and financial audits for the private and not-for-profit sectors. She subsequently returned to Texas, where she reestablished MMS and currently manages the firm, which now has offices in Austin, Dallas, and Fort Worth.

Marilou Martinez Stevens is an exemplar of resiliency. She is also an outstanding example of leadership in the Hispanic community throughout the United States. She contributes to her own community by teaching accounting classes at the Hispanic Chamber of Commerce, with the objective of educating Latino small business owners, so that they, too, learn to make sound business decisions.

Named as one of the most 100 Most Influential Hispanics in America, Marilou counts among her achievements past chair of the Texas Association of Mexican American Chambers of Commerce (TAMACC), the first female to hold the post in the organization's 25-year history. She is also one of the founders of the New America Alliance (NAA), and has served as treasurer and vice-chair of governance on the NAA board of directors for three years.

36

Live Big and Reach for the Stars

YSABEL DURON

Co-Anchor, KRON TV, San Francisco; Founder and Executive Director,
Latinas Contra Cancer

*The only failure is not trying, so it is important to always put in
all your effort, especially when trying to reach higher levels of success.*

If Ysabel Duron's life motto were printed on a bumper sticker, it would
read: "Live big and reach for the stars." Ysabel credits her "dream big"
philosophy to her mother, her role model. As a child, whenever she got
stuck on a problem, she knew who to turn to.

Ysabel and her five siblings grew up in the agricultural town of Salinas,
California. Her father's family had migrated there from Mexico in hopes
of finding more and better opportunities for themselves and their children. Ysabel's family lived in a small one-bedroom home, and her parents
had to sleep in the living room. But they didn't complain—what mattered
was that their children had a roof over their heads.

"Stand tall, and have a strong will."

Without a doubt, Ysabel's strongest influence was her mother. Only
five feet tall, this strong-willed woman, an Arizona native, worked hard in
the canneries so that she could provide a private Catholic school education for her children. She was the personification of determination and

resilience. Ysabel vividly remembers a pivotal moment that, she says, helped shape who she is today. One day, sitting at the kitchen table with her siblings doing homework and talking loudly with their mother, her father, who was sitting in the living room reading the paper, yelled out, "You kids think you're so smart; be quiet, or I'll take you out of that school!" Their mother yelled back, "No you won't! I pay for that school!" Twelve-year-old Ysabel took from that interchange the important realization that economic power gave you control. She extrapolated from that another important awareness, that without education, there would be no money, and without money, there would be no power over one's destiny.

"Economic power gives you control."

That Catholic school education her mother worked so hard to give Ysabel and her siblings also prepared them well for college. Eventually, she and two of her siblings graduated from the University of California, at Berkeley.

Today, Ysabel is an award-winning co-anchor on KRON, a San Francisco television news station. She says she has seen tremendous change in the more than three decades she has worked in the field of journalism—although she laments that the number of Latinos in the field is still currently less than 8 percent. Studies show that after five years in broadcasting, up to 50 percent of Latinos drop out because of discrimination, feelings of isolation, a lack of support, and, consequently, an inability to get ahead.

But Ysabel herself has been resilient. When she became one of the first Latinas to work in television in the San Francisco Bay Area, in 1970, she was dismayed to find she faced reverse discrimination. Other Latinos criticized her for working in the English-language media. Her position was that working in mainstream television would help change the societal stereotype of Latinos. She intended to prove that Latinos could be successful journalists, and she hoped to serve as a role model for other Latinos interested in similar careers.

Ysabel Duron has achieved her objectives, and then some. In 2005, she was named one of the 26 most influential Latinos in the San Francisco Bay Area. She is a member of the National Association of Hispanic

Journalists, and was named one of America's Top 100 Hispanic Women in Communications by *Hispanic USA* magazine. Ysabel is a board member of the International Women's Media Foundation, and of the Valley Medical Center Foundation in San Jose, California.

Ysabel also founded, three years ago, the nonprofit organization, Latinas Contra Cancer, to raise cancer awareness in the low-income, Spanish-speaking community, provide support services to cancer patients, and design basic educational tools for use around the country.

37

Connect with Your Culture

ALICIA MORGA
Founder and CEO, Consorte Media

Integrate your culture and passion in the workplace.

Alicia Morga is the founder of Consorte Media, an Internet marketing company whose mission is to connect advertisers with U.S. Hispanics online. To that end, the company runs a media network that gives Latino community members access to information and services they might not otherwise have. Consorte Media also operates Web sites that have helped countless Latinos buy their first cars and secure home loans, as well as influence decisions that have made a significant impact in their lives. Alicia says her company has also given her the opportunity to make other companies in the country aware that the Hispanic market is an important and steadily growing one and not to be overlooked.

"It is important for Latinos to be connected to technology to have access to opportunities."

Before starting Consorte Media, Alicia gained a wealth of experience through various positions in business and marketing. She was an investment professional focused on U.S. venture opportunities in the technology sector for the Carlyle Group's U.S. Venture Fund. Prior to joining Carlyle, Alicia was with Hummer Winblad Venture Partners, where her specialty was early-stage software investments. While at Hummer Winblad, Alicia also served as vice president of operations for Napster and chief executive officer of Zero Gravity Internet Group, Inc., a venture fund. Alicia has also worked as a corporate attorney for Wilson Sonsini Goodrich & Rosati, and in investment banking at Goldman Sachs.

Alicia has been a presence on the boards of several companies, as well, including Ingenio, Ventaso, Secure Elements, Archetype-Solutions, Applied Semantics, Menerva Technologies, Inc., and Discovercast, Inc.

In the course of building her career, however, the day came when Alicia realized she had become disconnected to her culture, when she realized that the only person she had spoken Spanish with in the last year was the woman who emptied the trash on her floor at work. "I started to wonder," she said, "how I could put together my passion for my culture with my work experience. I was fortunate enough to have a friend who became an entrepreneur at the same time, and he inspired me to find this connection in the online advertising world."

In retrospect, Alicia, a Mexican-American, is grateful for her modest upbringing, in a two-bedroom home that she shared with ten siblings in Los Angeles, California. She always had big dreams, however. One day inhigh school, her sister, Maria, read in *Seventeen* magazine that Stanford was the best school in California, so that's where Alicia decided she would go. She earned a bachelor's degree from that prestigious school, followed by a jurisprudence degree from Stanford Law School.

Today, Alicia Morga is an inspiration and role model for young Latinas. She recommends that anyone looking to pursue a career in the venture capital industry should first go to business school—"It's a great networking resource, since getting into the venture world is more about who you know." She also recommends to budding businesspeople that they gain operating experience at a company in the industry of interest—that is, if you want to be a tech venture capitalist, it's a good idea to work first at a tech company.

38

See the Big Picture

LUIS RESTREPO
CEO, Multitrade Securities

*Pursuing your dreams in America begins with creating a big picture
in your mind.*

Emigrating from Colombia, South America, to the United States
quickly made twelve-year-old Luis Restrepo aware that achieving
the American dream would be difficult, given his day-to-day reality in the
low-income housing projects of New York City, where he was exposed
to drugs, gangs, and violence. Here, he just as quickly realized, he would
have to work hard and be determined if he was to improve his situation
and live in a neighborhood with good public schools, youth centers, and
positive community involvement.

Like most immigrants to this country, his parents had to work long,
hard hours to provide for their family. And so, when his father and
mother were away from home, Luis, the oldest sibling, took on the role
of surrogate father to his four younger siblings. Luis saw how tired his
mother was when she came home from the sewing machine company—
in reality, a sweatshop—where she labored to give him and his brothers
and sisters the opportunity to make something more of their lives. He,
too, became resilient, studying hard and keeping his eye on the prize. His
focus paid off when his academic record caught the attention of a guidance counselor, who recognized the potential in this young man. The
counselor encouraged Luis to attend the best public school in New York,

Stuyvesant High School, well known for its math and science programs. But the process of getting into Stuyvesant was rigorous—thousands of children from around the five boroughs of New York apply, so the counselor helped Luis with the process. Of the select number of students accepted, Luis was one of the lucky ones.

"A great education pays off."

But his family now lived on Staten Island, so during his last three years of high school, Luis traveled three hours a day—by bus, ferry, and subway—to get a better education. After his long commute home again, Luis still was responsible for taking care of his siblings, so it was not until midnight or later that he could begin to study and do his homework for the advanced courses he was now taking.

Luis continued to do well, and when his high school counselor asked him which colleges he wanted to apply to, he replied, Harvard, Princeton, and Columbia. Luis was accepted by all three, but he chose to attend Harvard, which he was able to afford thanks to the scholarships he had won as a result of his outstanding academic record.

After he received his bachelor's degree, Luis worked for a couple of years before going on to one of the top-tier business schools in the country, the Wharton School at the University of Pennsylvania. From there, he received his master's in business administration.

Today, Luis is the chief executive officer of Multitrade Securities, a firm he founded in 1999 through a strategic alliance with Bloomberg and the Bank of New York. He also serves as a board member of the New America Alliance, the City Club of New York, and the Wharton Olympus club.

In addition, Luis remains an integral part of the Latino community. In particular, Luis believes strongly that it's important to expose young Latinos to positive role models in the community. He is concerned that too many of them seek out celebrities to emulate. Instead, Luis stresses, the Latino community must emphasize the value of a good education, if the next generation is to have the opportunity to aim for the top in all fields of endeavor.

39

Hope Is Always on Your Side

REVEREND LUIS A. CORTES, JR.
Founder and President, Esperanza USA

Transforming lives is a key element of growth and change.

Reverend Luis A. Cortes, Jr., grew up on 102nd Street, in the one of the projects of New York's Spanish Harlem. There, on the twentieth floor of a thirty-story building, he was surrounded by poverty, and all the misery that comes with it. Like so many others who had moved to the Big Apple, Luis's parents, who had emigrated from Puerto Rico, did so in hopes of providing a better life for their children, believing in all they'd heard about "the land of opportunity."

For young Luis, however, the despair he saw around him was met with a powerful rival: religion. Faith was to play a major part in his upbringing. He remembers his parents assuring him, *"Tenemos que paranos cuando callemos, Christo lo da lar fuerza para server."* ("Christ provides us with the strength for perseverance; therefore, we can always get up from failure.") While living in the projects, in addition to his supportive parents, Luis was also lucky to have two inspirational mentors: Dr. Soto-Fontanez, who received his PhD in Spanish Literature from Columbia University, and Reverend Dr. Orlando Costas, who was a young, energetic Puerto Rican theologian. Dr. Soto-Fontanez saw much strength in Luis—he had resiliency and the capacity and desire to learn. Each week, Dr. Soto-Fontanez would assign Luis a book to read, and later would meet with him to quiz him about what he had read and discuss the important messages of the book. But it was Dr. Orlando Costas, author of sixteen books himself, who introduced Luis to the Latin Seminary.

With these two inspirational mentors, Luis could not help but become motivated to go to college. After graduating with honors from City College in New York, he went on to earn a master of science in economic development from New Hampshire College, and, finally, a master of divinity as an urban theology fellow from Union Theological Seminary. It was this latter path Luis decided to follow. Seeing a need for community services and the growth of the Latino community in the greater Philadelphia area, Reverend Luis took the opportunity to open his heart and his doors and, in 1987, established Esperanza USA, a network that now comprises 10,000 Hispanic faith- and community-based agencies. This powerful organization now serves as one of the leading voices for Hispanics in the United States. It includes a charter high school, a junior college, homebuilding services, mortgage counseling, employment training programs, and a national HIV/AIDS education initiative. It is understandable why "esperanza," which means "hope" in Spanish, was chosen as the name for the organization.

"Christ provides us with the strength for perseverance; therefore, we can always get up from failure."

Recently, Esperanza USA embarked on $28-million economic development project to revitalize a Latino corridor in North Philadelphia, by transforming lots and abandoned buildings into a vibrant commercial area surrounded by new and renovated homes. In 2004, the organization launched *Esperanza Trabajando* (Hope Is Working), a three-year employment program for at-risk Latino youth. The project is supported by the U.S. Department of Labor, and has a budget of $11 million, which will be used to transform the lives of unemployed and misdirected youth in nine major cities in the country, by preparing them for specific careers. Ultimately, the project will expand to Chicago, Dallas, Denver, and Houston.

In January 2005, Reverend Cortes was featured as one of *TIME* magazine's 25 Most Influential Evangelicals. He was also asked to speak at the National Prayer Service the morning after President George W. Bush's inauguration. In the summer of 2005, Luis hosted the National Hispanic Prayer Breakfast, the largest gathering of Hispanic clergy in the United States, whose mission is to offer enlightenment and empowerment to clergy, community leaders, and policymakers. President Bush was there, too, lending his support.

Reverend Luis A. Cortes's mission is to pioneer other programs that will empower Hispanics into the twenty-first century. To that end, Esperanza USA continues to grow and make positive changes in the Hispanic community nationwide.

40

Always Push Yourself

ROBERTO MEDRANO
Executive Vice President of Sales and Marketing, Digital Evolution, SOA Software

When you work hard in life, good things happen.

Roberto Medrano will never forget the day he left Mexico City, alone, to move to Boyle Heights in East Los Angeles, California. He was just nineteen years old. Though he may have come alone, he carried with him the inspiration and encouragement of his mother to sustain him during his early days in his new surroundings. She told him to push *con fuerza*, with all his force, to succeed in his new environment. Roberto kept his mother's advice in mind, and pushed through to succeed by working hard in school in hopes of attending college one day.

"It's important to understand where you come from and where you want to go in life."

Once settled into his new home, Roberto enrolled in East Los Angeles Community College, where he went on to receive an associate of science degree in engineering. Even while working full-time, he earned straight A's in physics and mathematics, subjects difficult for many but which seemed to come easily to Roberto.

The dean of the Engineering Department, who saw incredible potential in Roberto, encouraged him to pursue his studies. Since he felt comfortable and happy in his community, and liked living among other Latinos in the barrio, he chose to remain in the area and go to the University of Southern California, where he received a bachelor of science degree in electrical engineering. After receiving honors in his undergraduate program, he decided to continue his academic career. For this he chose the prestigious Massachusetts Institute of Technology, where he received a master of science degree in electrical engineering. Then it was back to Los Angeles, where he attended the University of California, at Los Angeles, for the purpose of obtaining a master of business administration degree.

Now armed with two master's degrees and powerful motivation, Roberto was ready to break into the corporate world. He says, "It's imperative to aim high, never look back, and never see something as an obstacle, but as a challenge and an opportunity to succeed. It's important to understand where you come from and where you want to be in life."

He became president and CEO of Hispanic–Net, an organization created and led by Hispanic entrepreneurs, business executives, and other highly skilled professionals. Roberto's goal for the organization was to assist Hispanic entrepreneurs in the development of high-tech businesses, a field in which he is recognized internationally as an expert. Specifically, in the field of computer and Internet security, Roberto has helped develop firewalls, intrusion prevention software, and content security.

In addition, he has extensive experience with start-ups and large companies alike. Roberto has delivered an IPO and rounds of financing in three industries: electronic design automation, open systems, and computer security. Roberto was CEO of Polivec, a leader in security policy automation. Prior to Polivec, Roberto was one of the top one hundred senior executives at Hewlett Packard (HP). At HP, he was responsible for managing seven software development divisions, and served a vital role as head of HP's key strategic emerging businesses. He also led a number of initiatives that focused on developing new products and solutions designed to facilitate all aspects of electronic commerce. In September 2004, Medrano was named executive vice president of sales and marketing for Digital Evolution, where his job is to deliver innovative SOA Software solutions to an expanding customer base.

"Aim high, never look back, and never see something as an obstacle, but as a challenge and an opportunity to succeed."

Roberto travels the world educating leaders in business, government, and academia. Currently, he is a member of the National Security Advisory Council for President Bush, and is involved in the White House National Strategy to Secure Cyberspace. He participated in President Clinton's White House Security Summit, where he met with other influential technology industry leaders and senior White House administration and cabinet leaders. These meetings started an ongoing dialogue between the White House and the private sector, for the purpose of enhancing the security and reliability of the Internet

In 2001, Roberto was selected as one of the 100 Most Influential Hispanics by Hispanic–Net. He has received numerous awards for business and product achievement from leading business and industry publications, including *Fortune, Red Herring, PC Magazine, InfoWorld, Data Communications*, and many others. He has also published numerous articles and is widely quoted as an expert source.

As a Latino who has become a business leader, Roberto says, "It's important to have a Latino role model at an early age. It's also crucial to shape your own thinking by contributing to your community." He adds that, "In becoming successful in the business world, it's vital to be flexible, to know that at any moment you may have to relocate for that next managerial position. And always believe you have the talent to climb to the top. To be successful, it's important to understand the mainstream society in which you reside, adopt some of the values, acculturate them into your leadership role, and accept the responsibility of being a role model."

41

Life Experiences Create Strength

DANIEL GUTIERREZ
Author; Founder and CEO of Pinnacle Achievement Group International

Strength, determination, and perseverance will help you to get where you need to go in life.

Daniel Gutierrez started life faced with numerous challenges. When he was very young, his father was killed in a car accident. As a single parent, his mother made many sacrifices for Daniel and his siblings, laboring as a migrant worker in Dixon, California. For many years, the staple diet of Daniel's family was *queso, frijoles, tortillas,* and *juevos* (cheese, beans, tortillas, and eggs).

Daniel came to regard his mother as a source of inspiration; he says it was his mother's strength and determination in the face of countless hardships that motivated him to become the author and entrepreneur he is today. He also learned from her he would have to rely on his strength and inner drive to achieve greatness in whatever he chose to do.

"Success is born when our ability to focus on our dreams is greater than our fixation on our current problems."

Daniel went to college in Texas and started working for Best Buy as a general manager. At this Fortune 500 company, he learned to change challenging situations into win-win opportunities that would benefit the customers and help to promote his climb to the top of the corporate ladder. His vision was to enable Mexican citizens to obtain Best Buy credit cards, so they could then cross the border for the day and make purchases at Best Buy on credit. Daniel also began to devise creative ways to use Best Buy's power with this population to gain influence with the media both in the United States and Mexico. He captured the attention of *Diario de Juarez*, a newspaper in Juarez, Mexico, and established a relationship that benefited both the newspaper and Best Buy, by bringing in advertising dollars to the paper and new customers to Best Buy. This strategy increased the visibility of the store and gave Mexicans and Mexican–Americans the feeling that Best Buy valued their business.

Daniel's achievements at Best Buy led him to realize he wanted to become a Latino motivator in business and in life. "Success is up to you," Daniel writes in his book, *Stepping into Greatness* (Penmarin Books, 2005)."Successful people do what unsuccessful people aren't willing to do: work long hours, take risks, and hold in mind a dream until it happens. Of course these things take self-leadership and determination."

In 2002, Daniel was nominated for the 12th Annual *Hispanic Business Magazine* Entrepreneur Award, which recognizes the business owner who epitomizes the drive to succeed. Daniel found his inspiration and drive as a young man in the small, impoverished town of Midlothian, Texas, proving that success can have strong roots even in seemingly barren soil.

Today, Daniel is the CEO of the Pinnacle Achievement Group International. The company mission is to facilitate economic growth and to be a leader in building relationships as a catalyst in the global marketplace.

VI

EDUCATION

E ducation is a source of power, whether it is obtained through formal education or through life experiences. You cannot be successful without education. Even self-starters understand the value of educating themselves, of asking questions and gaining experience wherever they go. Self-education requires the discipline to teach yourself; formal education requires the discipline to apply yourself to your studies. To be successful, you will need either a degree from a university or a degree in applied life learning.

Education is tied to resiliency, the characteristic that develops as a result of having to prove yourself over and over, which requires patience, persistence, and the ability to bounce back from challenges or failures. The formal education system is built on this principle. Students are required repeatedly to demonstrate that they have the capacity to learn and can overcome disappointment. Once they have gained knowledge and learned the new skills, they must pass inspection, whether in the form of exams, research papers and projects, or internships. Both the formal education system and the school of hard knocks teach you to stick with it, whatever your *it* is.

Obviously, not everyone in life is fortunate enough to have access to a formal education. But with resiliency, coupled with a desire and willingness to learn in any environment, all motivated individuals can be just as successful as those who do. Opportunities for education surround all of us, everyday; but the most important opportunity is the one available to everyone: to learn about our own unique strengths, and how to build on them. Some will learn what they need to succeed in classroom; others will learn from a mentor who is an industry expert; some may even receive guidance from a how-to book.

Once you have learned all you need to achieve your goals, don't forget to share the wealth—perpetuate your success by sharing with others, by passing along what you've learned. Teaching others builds confidence, both in the teacher and the student. Build on your relationships, and be a sounding board for your peers and colleagues. Be a mentor to an up-and-coming performer in your organization, or join a community outreach mentoring program.

42

Listen, Learn, and Educate

RICARDO FERNANDEZ, PhD

President, Lehman College, City University of New York

The mission is to encourage more Latinos and other minorities to pursue a higher level of education.

Ricardo Fernandez was born and raised in Puerto Rico, along with his 10 brothers and sisters. He was fortunate to be sent to a Catholic school for boys, where he received a wonderful education. And when it was time to apply for college, a school priest advised him to attend a college in middle America, if he really wanted to learn about the United States. He took the priest's advice and was accepted to Marquette University, a Catholic school in Milwaukee, Wisconsin. There he received an undergraduate degree in philosophy and a graduate degree in Spanish.

Moving from Puerto Rico to Wisconsin in the early 1960s was, for Ricardo, a cultural and environmental shock. He went from spending hot, sunny days on beautiful sandy beaches to plowing through knee-deep snow on his walk to campus. But he had no regrets about his move, and quickly immersed himself in American culture. In particular, he loved baseball (he was an accomplished pitcher, himself) and became an ardent fan of the Milwaukee Braves (now the Atlanta Braves).

Baseball was more than just sport for him; it also was the venue in which he learned the value of teamwork and discipline, which helped him to stay focused on his schoolwork. After obtaining his master's degree,

Ricardo decided to pursue a doctoral degree in Romance languages and literature at Princeton University; subsequently, he attended the Harvard Institute for Educational Management.

Ricardo says his inspiration to succeed in academia came from his parents, who instilled in him as a young child the importance of a good education, and whose actions spoke as loud as their words—his father attended medical school in Puerto Rico, and his mother received her GED as an adult.

Ricardo's rise in the academic world began at Marquette University, where he was an assistant professor in Spanish, and later a professor in the Department of Educational Policy and Community Studies. Soon after, Ricardo became vice chancellor for academic affairs at the University of Wisconsin–Milwaukee. As one of only a few Latinos in academia at the time, Ricardo was even more motivated to reach for the top, and then to encourage other minority students to follow in his footsteps.

"The harder I work, the luckier I get."

In 1990, Ricardo became the president of the City University of New York's Lehman College, a liberal arts college and one of the nation's leading urban public universities. CUNY, with a student body of more than 10,000 from the metropolitan area, as well as 80 foreign countries, offers more than 90 undergraduate and graduate programs. Doctoral programs are offered through the graduate school and University Center, except for laboratory-based programs, which are offered through the individual colleges. And in association with the New York Botanical Garden, Lehman also offers a plant sciences program. Lehman College also sponsors more than 100 collaborative programs that provide assistance to Bronx public schools.

Ricardo is passionate about understanding the special needs and circumstances of Hispanic and other minority students. To that end, he has published books and research reports about the school dropout rate of this population, the desegregation of Hispanic students, and bilingual education policy.

Ricardo is proud to be president of Lehman College, and to be making a difference in the lives of Hispanic and other minority students. He leads by example, proving that it pays to be persistent in life, to apply lessons from past experiences, and to believe in the luck that hard work brings.

43

Aim for the Top

DAVID GARCIA, PhD
Founder and CEO, CEDRA Corporation

Passion should come straight from the heart.

Today, Dr. David Garcia is the founder and CEO of CEDRA Corporation. As a young boy growing up in the Escarate neighborhood in El Paso, Texas, he never dreamed he would one day be the head of a large pharmaceutical company.

Sadly, David's father, a native of Chihuahua, Mexico, died before he was born. So David was raised by his mother, with the help of his four older brothers. In particular, Enrique, fourteen years his senior, was like a father figure to him, says David. Enrique was also the fix-it man around the house, taking care of the plumbing and electrical needs in the home. In this way, he taught David the important lesson that things could be fixed when they weren't working, that people could sort out almost anything, if they put their minds to it. From his mother, David learned the importance of spirituality and honesty.

Not a good student in high school, after graduation, David was drafted into the Marine Corps and served in the Vietnam War. It turned out to be a fortunate turn of events, for it was in the military that David found meaning in life. After proudly serving his country, he became inspired him to go back to school, where he took math and chemistry courses. His excellent work in these studies further encouraged him, and he went on to apply to the University of Texas at El Paso, where he took prepharmacy courses for two years.

"Serving your country gives you an appreciation for life and teaches that it should not be taken for granted."

David later transferred to the University of Texas at Austin (UT), where he continued his pharmacy focus. There he caught the eye of Dr. Jaime N. Delgado, who became David's mentor. Recognizing that David's strength was in science lab courses, he encouraged David to apply for graduate school at UT. In 1977, David received his PhD in pharmaceutical chemistry. This was a dream come true for David, who at that time was the only one in his family to graduate from college. Later, David's older sister was inspired by the success of her younger brother, went back to school in her fifties, and obtained her teaching credentials.

Now, David runs CEDRA, which offers analytical, toxicology/pharmacology, metabolic, and synthetic chemistry, as well as pharmacokinetic/statistical services. But David offers another kind of service that is just as valuable. He is a mentor to many young Latinos, advising them how to go about achieving their dreams. David lives by the words, "I always get what I want," and tries to instill that belief in others—stressing that any goal is obtainable, if you try.

44

Communication Is a Powerful Tool

FEDERICO SUBERVI, PhD
Professor, School of Journalism and Mass Communication, Texas State University

Communication helps to bridge the gap in disenfranchised neighborhoods.

D r. Federico Subervi lived in Puerto Rico until the age of seven,
when his mother relocated the family to the Lower East Side of
Manhattan. Federico's mother was his hero and his inspiration in life, and
she made sure that he knew there was something better for him outside
of their *vecidario*, their neighborhood. She worked in sweatshops to support her family and made sacrifices to ensure that her children could finish their education and make a name for themselves.

"The world is bigger than this little neighborhood."

Growing up, Federico did not realize he was poor—all around him
were others in similar circumstances. Nor did his see himself as different, not until he was old enough to begin to analyze and understand the
differences between his reality and the one portrayed in popular media.
He began to wonder, Where are the Latinos? They weren't characters on
the television programs he watched, except in lesser roles as sidekicks or,
more commonly, villains.

Federico's role model was his uncle, Dr. Ismael Velez, a university
professor of botany. When Federico was eleven years old, he remembers

his uncle visiting his family and hanging a blanket on the wall to serve as a makeshift movie screen, on which he showed slides of all the places around the world he had traveled. Federico saw exciting images from Southeast Asia, South America, and Europe, and he became acutely aware that the world was a much bigger place than the barrio.

Later, Federico would find another role model in Dr. Luis Nieves Falcón, one of his college professors, who introduced him to the book, *The Colonizer and the Colonized*, by Albert Memmi. From this, Federico learned about the oppression and struggles of Puerto Ricans, and faced the fact that, to many, being Puerto Rican was the equivalent of being a second-class citizen. This awareness gave Federico the impetus for his personal mission: to tap into his own power and then to help other Latinos to empower themselves by becoming educated. He used as inspiration the insightful writings of Abrahim Maslow and the theory of self-actualization.

Upon completing his doctoral degree from the University of Wisconsin, Federico's goal was to make changes in international media. In Brazil, he helped reverse the negative portrayals of blacks in Brazil's television commercials. In Puerto Rico, his home country, Federico was the first person to systematically analyze the mass media systems, which became a useful tool for Latinos working in the field.

From 1982 to 1989, Federico taught at the University of California, Santa Barbara's Department of Communication, his first teaching job. He then went on to the University of Texas, where he was a professor at the Department of Radio-TV-Film and served as graduate advisor from 1989 to 2002. From 2002 to 2003, he became professor and chair of the Department of Communication Studies at Pace University in New York City. He has also been a UNESCO professor at the Universidad Metodista de São Paulo, Brazil, and visiting professor at the Universidad Diego Portales in Santiago, Chile, and the University of Amsterdam.

Federico now lives in Austin, Texas, where he is a media consultant and scholar. He also directs the Latinos and Media Project, an emerging nonprofit organization dedicated to the collection and dissemination of research and resources pertaining to Latinos and the media. For over twenty years, he has been teaching, conducting research, and publishing books and papers on issues pertaining to the mass media and ethnic groups, especially Latinos, in the United States. He is currently finishing a book on the mass media and Latino politics.

In addition to his academic work, Federico serves on editorial boards and has been an advisor or consultant to various public and private entities, such as Nickelodeon, Scholastic Entertainment, the Corporation for Public Broadcasting, Spanish Broadcasting System, Fox Family Worldwide, the National Research Council & Ford Foundation Fellowship Program, the National Latino Children's Institute, and Mothers Against Drunk Driving. He is also proud to serve as chair of the Board of Directors for Latinitas, Inc., a Web-based magazine for Latino teens.

45

Motivate Employees to Success

SARA MARTINEZ TUCKER
Former President and CEO, Hispanic Scholarship Fund

You must have the support of a network to succeed.

Sara Martinez Tucker, a native of Laredo, Texas, attributes her success to her supportive parents, especially her mother, who continually encouraged Sara and her siblings to do well in high school and go to college. All the Tucker children went on to earn college degrees. Sara's was in journalism, followed by an MBA from the University of Texas at Austin.

Sara believes that it is important to set high expectations for all Latinos. She says, "The first piece of advice I give to fellow Latinos is to go for the hard jobs that have quantifiable objectives, so that the results are subject to anybody's qualifications."

Sara also has a unique view on mentors. She believes they come in two types: those who offer long-range advice that you can apply throughout life, and those who are experts on the day-to-day work and whose advice is applicable on a more short-term basis. She also contends that some of the best mentors are tormentors. Whereas some, maybe most, people view tormentors as those who breathe down the necks of others, or give them very little space in which to be creative and thrive at work, she sees tormentors as those who are tough and have very little patience for failure. Thus, Sara believes that a boss who is both a tormentor as well as a mentor may receive more effective results. Early in her career, Sara decided she preferred a boss who is a tormentor. Sara, therefore, encourages people to look for mentors who are secure and confident, because these are the individuals who will give honest feedback. Most people don't want to hear criticism, but Sara prefers it. She thinks it is best for someone to be hard on her, as it helps her to grow and improve.

"Lead by example."

This tough approach seems to be working for her. In 1990, Sara became the first Latino to be promoted to AT&T's executive level. She was responsible for AT&T's Global Business Communications Systems, where profits soared to $400 million under her management. Prior to holding this position, she was vice president of consumer operations, a $370 million business with 6,500 employees serving AT&T's 80 million consumers. Sara has also served on the board of the National Hispanic Scholarship Foundation, the AT&T Foundation, the University of Texas Natural Sciences Advisory Council, and the Bay Area Council. These are important affiliations, because they give Sara the opportunity to give back to the Hispanic community.

In 1997, Sara was named president and CEO of the Hispanic Scholarship Fund (HSF), the nation's leading organization supporting higher education for Hispanic youth. This position was a natural fit for Sara. As a young girl growing up in a lower-income neighborhood, she suffered from a lack of resources and positive role models, and vowed that once she became successful, she would find a way to give back to the community. Since becoming president of the HSF, Sara has focused on doubling the rate of Hispanics earning college degrees. She is also responsible for securing $50 million in grants from the Lilly Endowment Inc., the largest direct gift ever granted for Hispanic higher education. During its twenty-nine-year history, HSF has awarded more than 66,000 scholarships, totaling more than $144 million, to deserving students at more than 1,700 universities and colleges throughout the United States, Puerto Rico, Guam, and the U.S. Virgin Islands.

Sara's outstanding work is widely recognized. She is the recipient of numerous awards, including being named one of *Hispanic Business* magazine's 100 Most Influential Hispanics in 1999. In 2000, *Hispanic Magazine* named her Hispanic of the Year. *Hispanic Business Magazine* also named Sara one of the 80 Elite Hispanic Women. In March 2002, readers of the online magazine, Hispanicsonline.com, honored her with the Latino Choice Award for Favorite Hispanic Leader.

In 2001, President George W. Bush appointed her to the board of directors of the government-sponsored student loan marketing association, commonly known as Sallie Mae. During the same year, Sara joined the North American Diversity Advisory Board of Toyota Corporation. The goal of her participation was to raise employee awareness of ethnic and minority issues, and to inform and consult the company on race relations in North America. Most recently, Sara was nominated by President Bush, and subsequently confirmed by the U.S. Senate, as Under Secretary of Education.

46

Hispanics on the Move

JOSE ANTONIO TIJERINO
President and CEO, Hispanic Heritage Foundation

There is a trend of Latinos breaking barriers in the workplace.

Jose Antonio Tijerino came to the United States with his parents as a young child. As a native of Nicaragua, his first challenge, as for many Spanish-speaking immigrants to this country, was to learn to speak English. Fortunately, he had the support of his family and the determination to do well in school. His high school, he says was culturally diverse; and though he was sometimes thought to be Italian, Jose Antonio always proudly announced he was a Latino from Nicaragua.

Jose Antonio went on to pursue a bachelor of science degree in journalism, with a minor in psychology from the University of Maryland. Upon graduation, he started his professional career in communications and marketing. He became aware quickly, however, that the general perception of Latinos in the professional community was another challenge he would have to meet, repeatedly. He remembers attending a black tie event at which a white man, mistaking Jose Antonio for a member of the valet staff of the hotel, tossed him his car keys and asked him to fetch it.

In his rise to the upper ranks of his profession, Jose Antonio worked in increasingly responsible positions. As an account supervisor at, first, Burson–Marsteller and, then, Cohn & Wolf, public relations firms in Washington, he developed and managed public relations and public affairs campaigns. He moved on to Nike, Inc., where he was a manager for corporate communications in the marketing department. His next job was as director of public relations in the communications department for the Fannie Mae Foundation. In 2001, Jose Antonio became the president and CEO of the Hispanic Heritage Foundation (HHF), where he oversees the operations of this national, nonprofit organization.

"Never waste time focusing on stereotypes."

According to the Department of Labor, over the next fifteen years, more than two-thirds of the growth in the American workforce will be Latino, but less than 1 percent of those workers will be in management positions. In light of this startling discrepancy, the HHF, in partnership with the Hispanic College Fund, created Latinos On the Fast Track (LOFT), with the objective of systematically identifying, preparing, and placing next-generation Latino professionals in industry-specific jobs, to bolster the Latino management presence in America's workforce.

Through partnerships in the private and public sectors, LOFT identifies appropriate candidates for targeted jobs or internships, and provides industry-specific training through tutorials, workshops, and educational materials. This close attention to every step in the employment process not only prepares future leaders but also motivates the candidates to have an immediate impact and perform at a high level. These tailored programs also are intended to improve communities with the presence of Latinos in various industries, including mortgage lending, engineering, technology, private banking, insurance, homebuilding, retail, and even the entertainment industry.

HHF also has launched a Leadership Luncheon series, at which young leaders are invited to discuss current issues, learn about opportunities available in numerous industries, and gain a better understanding of the types of jobs available. These luncheons also help prepare LOFT members for entrance into the workforce and to take advantage of leadership opportunities.

Jose Antonio is also extremely active in the District of Columbia community, where he serves on several boards and as communications counsel to numerous nonprofits. In addition, he is a member of Mayor Anthony Williams' Commission on Latino Affairs.

47

Answering the Spiritual Calling

Dr. Ana Maria Pineda
Professor of Religious Studies, Santa Clara University

The passion to help others must come naturally, and from the heart.

A na Maria Pineda was born in San Salvador, El Salvador. At the age of two, she and her family immigrated to the United States, settling in the Mission District in San Francisco, California. Ana Maria always understood who she was as a child, for her parents encouraged her to always do her best, and taught her the value of compassion for those less privileged. She knew early that her mission in life would be to help others, and felt strongly that God wanted her to give her life to His service, and specifically, to the Latino community in this country.

Ana Maria believes that an essential part of life is to connect with the inner self, and to understand all the intricacies in life, in order to become spiritual, spontaneous, and intuitive.

"Never shut the door on opportunity; open your eyes to new possibilities."

From 1979 to 1985, Ana Maria was a doctor of ministry degree candidate at the Jesuit School of Theology at the Graduate Theological Union in Berkeley. She then went to the Catholic Theological Union in Chicago, where she earned her master's in theology, in 1987. Five years later, she completed her degree in pastoral theology from the Universidad Pontificia de Salamanca, Spain. Her dissertation examined the Hispanic permanent deaconate in the United States.

Ana Maria joined the Santa Clara University (SCU) faculty in 1997. She was the first Latina professor in the Religious Studies Department, where she teaches courses on Hispanic spirituality and theology, which attract many Latino as well as non-Latino students. One of her most popular courses is TESP 109: Our Lady of Virgin Guadalupe. Guadalupe is a powerful and loving presence in the Mexican community, a symbol—a presence, really—who stands as a sign of hope, and a reminder that it is possible to overcome difficulties and to forge a better tomorrow for all. Notably, today, other professors throughout the country are teaching the religious and spiritual significance, and sacred meaning, of the Virgin of Guadalupe.

Ana Maria's first major project at SCU was to collaborate with others on campus to link the Sacred Heart Parish Teatro Corazon with the university and her course on Our Lady of Virgin Guadalupe class. It turned out to be the beginning a ten-year tradition, in which the reenactment of Our Lady of Guadalupe to the Mission Church is performed annually. Students from Ana Maria's class visit the Teatro Corazon members at Sacred Heart Parish and discover why Guadalupe is so important to the Latino community. This exchange confirms and enriches the content of Ana Maria's course and forges lasting relationships with the community of Sacred Heart Parish. In the second year of the collaboration, the Juan Diego Scholarship program was established to enable a student from Sacred Heart parish to attend SCU for four years.

In 1998, Ana Maria's class on U.S. Hispanic Popular Religiosity was instrumental in the creation of the Altar of Remembrance tradition in the Mission Church, whose purpose is to help parishioners remember loved ones who have died. The altar, which remains in place throughout the month of November, has come to be an annual event that is much anticipated by community members.

48

Instilling Faith in Lower-Income Communities

LEO CHAVEZ
President/Superintendent, Sierra College, Rocklin, California

Participating in philanthropy is an uplifting experience.

Leo Chavez remembers growing up in an El Paso, Texas barrio as an experience that made him realize the significance of studying hard and doing well academically. He had the good fortune to attend a Jesuit high school that boasted a rich curriculum. At the same time, unfortunately, lines were clearly drawn between members of the student body based on ethnicity—the Hispanics and non-Hispanics each formed cliques, leading to a segregation few seemed to question.

Leo, however, was not one of them. Overcoming any fears he may have had, he began to "cross the line," determined to get to know his non-Hispanic fellow students. His natural curiosity and general interest in them—their culture, traditions, and families—enabled him to better understand life outside the barrio, and helped him to become more confident in the world at large. Over time, Leo became empowered, and began to make friends and build allegiances with non-Hispanics, which gave him the confidence he would need to succeed at the college level.

As it turned out, Leo's natural approach to challenges—to face fears and overcome obstacles by asking questions—became the foundation of his professional success. But first he would build on his strengths by completing his education: he received a bachelor of arts in history from the University of Texas, El Paso (which later awarded Leo the distinguished

Golden Nugget Award). He later earned both his master of arts and doctoral degrees from the University of Michigan, Ann Arbor.

Now fully prepared, Leo moved to the Santa Clara Valley in California—now known as Silicon Valley—to begin his academic career. He taught at San Jose City College, where he was the vice president of instruction for thirteen years, before becoming the president of West Valley College for six years; thereafter, he spent eight years as chancellor of DeAnza/Foothill College. Today, Leo is the president/superintendent of Sierra Community College in Rocklin, California.

Leo also worked as the executive vice president of the Community Foundation of Silicon Valley, which attends to the needs of Latino communities similar to the barrio he grew up in. The focus of the organization is to increase philanthropy in these areas by addressing such important issues as health, housing, and education, key factors to boosting the morale of any community and improving the future for next-generation Latinos

In addition, Leo has also served on the boards of the Executive Officers of the California Community Colleges, the Organization Center for Excellence in Nonprofits, the Good Samaritan Hospital, the Commission of Athletics for Community Colleges, and Silicon Valley United Way. Currently, he sits on the board of CoAmerica Bank.

49

Build Confidence in Latinos

Elva D. Diaz
Assistant Professor, University of California, Davis

Set high expectations from grade school through college.

Elva Diaz grew up in San Jose, California, where she attended public schools. Her parents encouraged her educational interests, knowing that as a young Latina she would need a good education to achieve her goals, whatever they might be.

Elva always had what it took to succeed: family support and the aspiration to be the best. These advantages stood her in good stead when she encountered the inevitable roadblocks. In her case, this meant lack of access to the advanced placement courses she wanted to take, in particular, advanced calculus. Undeterred, she traveled miles from her assigned high school, Silver Creek, to one that offered what she needed. There, too, Elva was head of the class. And at Silver Creek, Elva's longstanding interest in science was encouraged by her biology teacher, Mr. Mark Okuda, whose genuine interest in her was a major factor in helping her succeed in school. Mr. Okuda, who created a research-based classroom setting, gave Elva the confidence she needed to excel. And excel she did, maintaining a 4.0 GPA all four years, which led to the honor of graduating valedictorian of her class.

Elva went on to receive her bachelor's degree in biochemistry from Harvard University, where she graduated cum laude, followed by a PhD from Stanford University, also in biochemistry. While at Stanford, Elva encouraged teachers from nearby Andrew Hill High School to attend a summer research-based science program at the university, so that students in the teaching credentials program there could learn to incorporate more challenging techniques in their science curricula.

To this day, Elva says her academic success derives from the strong role models she had in her parents, and she remains ever mindful of their encouragement and support. She believes that having someone in your life who encourages you and promotes the importance of higher education is vital to fulfilling professional and personal dreams. It is, therefore, not surprising that, today, as a faculty member at the University of California, Davis, Elva is involved in identifying the most promising applicants for admission to the graduate programs there. She reads and reviews all applications, and interviews prospective students during recruitment week. Elva is also a member of a planning committee, whose objective is to encourage students to apply to the graduate program. She also enjoys being a role model for prospective Latino students, who might otherwise be discouraged from applying to graduate school.

"Science is matter of life's passion."

Elva also serves as a mentor for minority scientists through the Society of Neuroscience. There she pairs up with a student, typically another Latino, and encourages him or her to attend annual board meetings of the society. Her goal is to guide the student's career, and ultimately encourage him or her to give back to field of academia.

CONCLUSION

The profiles in this book are clear indicators of the upward mobility of Latinos in this country, thanks to their increasing access to enrichment and advocacy programs. These programs, such as the Hispanic Scholarship Fund, the National Society of Hispanic MBAs, New America Alliance, HACE, and the Hispanic Association for Corporate Responsibility, are empowering Latinos to take their rightful place in all areas of mainstream America. Many of the people interviewed for this book were the first in their families to graduate from college and the first in their generation to work in corporate America. Their stories show how they integrated their core values and leadership principles with their work ethic, while remaining true to their cultural heritage. In this way, this book also exemplifies how to guide and shape leadership in the workplace, whether in a private or private company, a Fortune 500 or Fortune 1000 firm, a government agency, or a nonprofit organization.

According to the *2005 Hispanic Almanac*, the Hispanic population grew faster than the general population, increasing from 35.3 million in April 2000 to 39.9 million in July 2003, thereby comprising 13 percent of the general population. It has also been reported that the rate of growth of this population as a whole was 2.5 percent. Since April 1, 2000, based on estimates of race and place of origin, Hispanics totaled 3.5 million, fully one-half the population growth of 6.9 million in the United States. Likewise, Hispanics are entering the U.S. labor force in record numbers, and have become an increasingly vital factor in the growth of the national economy.

The Bureau of Labor Statistics also projects that by 2010, employees of Hispanic origin will comprise 13 percent of the U.S. labor market (Fullerton & Toosi), making this minority group the largest. As you have read in the book, Latinos in American represent a wide variety of national origins, ethnic and cultural groups, and social classes.

More statistics about this vital population comes from Rogelio Saenz, professor and head of the Department of Sociology at Texas A&M University, and author of numerous journal articles, book chapters, and technical reports on the demography of Latinos, immigration, social inequality, and race and ethnicity. His works shows that over the last several decades, the racial and ethnic composition of the U.S. population has changed markedly. Minorities in general are increasing their presence in the United States, and will continue to do so for the foreseeable future, but none more so than the Latino population. Today, one of every eight residents of the United States is Latino, and it is projected this population could account for one of every five residents by 2035, one of every four by 2055, and one of every three by 2100.

Latinos are already having a significant impact on all segments of society in the United States. Today, Latinos are critical to the future social and economic direction of the United States. Furthermore, transnational migration has blurred international and identity boundaries. Immigration has blurred the boundaries associated with nativity, even within families. The dominance of Spanish language instruction in colleges and universities, and its increasing presence in mainstream popular culture, also is serving to erase language boundaries.

U.S. institutions will increasingly be affected by and become dependent on Latinos in the coming decades. The business community will increasingly rely on Latinos as entrepreneurs, employees, investors, and consumers. The higher education system will increasingly find

Latinos among the ranks of both students and educators. Political institutions will find Latinos playing a more powerful role in the outcome of elections, both as voters and as political candidates. The health care system will recognize Latinos as health care recipients and providers. Religious institutions will find that their potential adherents and leaders will come more often from the Latino population.

In conclusion, there can be no doubt that the Latino population is, and will continue to be, a valuable resource for this country.

ACKNOWLEDGMENTS

FRANK CARBAJAL—To my wife, Molly: Thank you for your support and assistance with this book. Without you, my dreams would not have come to fruition. Thank you, too, for giving me our three beautiful daughters, Alia, Myla, and Bria.

To my daughter Myla: Your near-death experience and fight to stay with us on this earth has demonstrated true resiliency and taught me how to keep things in perspective. Despite your diagnosis of severe spastic quadriplegia cerebral palsy, you continue to smile and shower your love upon those around you. I would also like to thank the staff at the Benjamin Bloom Hospital in El Salvador, for saving Myla's life, and the staff at the Santa Clara Valley Medical Center in San Jose, California, for keeping Myla healthy. My gratitude also goes out to the Scribbles and Giggles Pediatric Day Health Center in Saratoga, California, Myla's many therapists, and her "angels," Cecilia Aviles-Fisher and Michele "Miggy" Tatos.

To my parents, Regino and Hermelinda: Thank you for teaching me to work hard and to have in faith in God.

To my siblings, Jisela, Ray, Maria, and Diana: Thank you for always believing in me; and to Hermelinda Negrette, who has always been like a sister to me.

To my nieces and nephews: Remember to study hard, believe in yourselves, and follow your dreams.

To my mother-in-law, Estela Gonzales: Thank you for taking care of my daughters and teaching them Spanish.

To the following individuals who have inspired me from beginning: Miguel "Michael" Bennett, Mark Villareal, Clay Deanhart, my godparents—Vicante and Licha Perez, Mr. Jackson, Oscar Zavaleta, Gil Villagran, Harold Leffal, Kimberly Fulcher, Bruce Walthers, Michael Garber, Daniel Gutierrez, Mike Garcia, Alex Ontiveros, Robert Rodriguez, Raymond Arroyo, Jimmy Hill, and Evie Cruz.

To the staff at The Ken Blanchard Management Company: Thank you for your support—especially, Nancy Jordan, who saw the potential in my book and connected me to Anna Espino. Anna, you have been the eyes and ears of this project and I appreciate you from the bottom of my heart. I thank you for introducing me to my awesome coauthor, Humberto Medina. Thanks also to Richard Andrews and Martha Lawrence, for your expertise.

To our editors at John Wiley & Sons, Inc., Emily Conway, Miriam Palmer-Sherman, and Christine Kim in marketing: Thank you for your patience and giving us an opportunity to live our dreams and to make this book a reality.

And last, to the National Society of Hispanic MBAs (NSHMBA), Silicon Valley chapter and members nationwide: Live your dreams and never forget the *frijoles* (beans).

HUMBERTO MEDINA—To my wife, Debbie, who has always supported my dreams and is my source of inspiration. And to my son Alec, who is a treasure of happiness and always brings a smile to my face.

To my parents, who always said that I would achieve great things in life. To my dad for being a great role model and for his hard work and dedication; and to my mom for her never-ending love and trust in me. To my grandparents, who thought I was special and were always proud of me.

To my sisters, Maru and Paty, who believed that I could make it in the United States or anywhere.

To Ken Blanchard and Majorie Blanchard, thank you for all of your love, insight, wisdom, and support. To my dear friend Drea Zigrami, for his continued support and for making me believe that I could do this project. To Richard Andrews, who always looked after me and played a key role in making this book happen.

To Briana and Anna Espino, you have always believed in me and were there to carry me through this project. To you I give special thanks for making me a better person every time I'm with you, and for working on this book. Thanks for believing in my leadership.

Finally, we both would like to also acknowledge the following individuals who participated as interviewees in our book. Maria del Pilar Avila, Eddie Correra, Ron Gonzales, Jorge Gonzalez, Sandra Milan, Cesar Plata, Jaime Quevedo, Hank Rosendin, Olga Talamante, and Carrie Zepeda. You all are great role models.